THE RESUME HANDBOOK

Fourth Edition

THE RESUME HANDBOOK

How to Write Outstanding Resumes & Cover Letters for Every Situation

Fourth Edition

Arthur D. Rosenberg
& David Hizer

ADAMS MEDIA CORPORATION
Avon, Massachusetts

Dedication

Sadly, Dave Hizer is no longer able to share with us his insights and guidance. I owe Dave a debt of gratitude for his years of contributions and commitment. Ours was a true collaboration of talents and effort, and the fourth edition of *The Resume Handbook* is my humble offering to his memory.

Heartfelt thanks to Sara Hizer, to my wife, Catherine, and to the Adams Media editorial staff, for your support and encouragement.

Published by
Adams Media, an F+W Publications Company
57 Littlefield Street, Avon, MA 02322 U.S.A.
www.adamsmedia.com

ISBN: 1-58062-854-0

Printed in Canada.

J   I   H   G   F   E   D

Library of Congress Cataloging-in-Publication Data
Rosenberg, Arthur D.
The resume handbook / Arthur D. Rosenberg and David Hizer.-- 4th ed.
p.   cm.
ISBN 1-58062-854-0
1. Resumes (Employment) I. Hizer, David V. II. Title.

HF5383.R67 2003
650.14'2--dc21

2003004613

This publication is designed to provide accurate and authoritative information with regard to the subject matter covered. It is sold with the understanding that the publisher is not engaged in rendering legal, accounting, or other professional advice. If legal advice or other expert assistance is required, the services of a competent professional person should be sought.

— From a *Declaration of Principles* jointly adopted by a Committee of the American Bar Association and a Committee of Publishers and Associations

Many of the designations used by manufacturers and sellers to distinguish their products are claimed as trademarks. Where those designations appear in this book and Adams Media was aware of a trademark claim, the designations have been printed with initial capital letters.

This book is available at quantity discounts for bulk purchases.
For information, call 1-800-872-5627.

About the Authors

Art Rosenberg is a New York/New Jersey–based consultant specializing in business analysis, project management, user-friendly documentation, corporate communications, and training. His publications include: *Career Busters: 22 Ways People Mess Up Their Careers and How to Avoid Them* (McGraw-Hill); *Manipulative Memos: Control Your Career Through the Medium of the Memo* (Ten Speed Press); contributed chapters to *The Requirements of Programming and Preparing for a Successful Interview* (McGraw-Hill) and to *Chess for Children and the Young at Heart* (Atheneum); and numerous articles.

Art is a former textbook publisher, translator, and language teacher who continues to provide career-related seminars to professional and minority groups. His eclectic interests include sports, chess, wines, fine dining, travel, music, and good books.

Dave Hizer was a Detroit-based executive search consultant who dedicated his efforts to matching talented executives with his clients' organizations. He brought more than thirty years of experience in executive searches, organizational development, public speaking, human resources, and outplacement to his profession.

Dave used to read more resumes per week than the number of newspaper headlines skimmed by most people in a year. He authored countless articles on career planning, self-marketing strategies, and related topics, including "The ABC's of Cover Letters" *(National Business Employment Weekly)*. He also made time to conduct frequent workshops and seminars on leadership and career/life planning.

Contents

Preface ix

Introduction xi

Chapter One:
Looking for a New Job 1

Chapter Two:
The Basic Principles of Resume Writing 5

Chapter Three:
Stating Your Accomplishments 9

Chapter Four:
The Best Resumes We've Ever Seen 19

Chapter Five:
The Five Worst Resumes We've Ever Seen 73

Chapter Six:
Presentation 91

Chapter Seven:
Using the Internet 97

Chapter Eight:
The Art of Networking 103

Chapter Nine:
Advice for Job Seekers 111

Chapter Ten:
Cover Letters. 115

Chapter Eleven:
Personal Promo Letters. 127

Chapter Twelve:
Following Up 133

Chapter Thirteen:
Other Job Search Methods 137

Afterword 145

Preface

The purpose of a resume is to *obtain an interview*.

Your resume is your official representative, a verbal portrait calculated *to arouse an important person's interest in meeting you*.

Your resume is not an autobiographical profile; it's a marketing piece on you. It isn't intended to make people like you or admire you.

Think of your resume as a special tool with one specific purpose: *winning an interview*.

That's right, you've got to go out and *win* your interview, and only the inexperienced and the naïve think otherwise. Your resume is a tool designed to get your foot in the doors of companies where you'd like to work. And if you fail to win the interview, you certainly won't get the job.

But there are other resumes out there in competition with your own. So yours must be at least as good as all the others if you're to stand an even chance. Of course, if your resume is *better* it may give you the advantage.

To write an interview-winning resume, you need to know what to say, and how to say it. For this, you need *The Resume Handbook*.

Just as the purpose of your resume is to obtain the interview, the purpose of *The Resume Handbook* is to illustrate successful resume techniques.

The Resume Handbook tells you what kind of information to include in your resume, and what to leave out. Then it provides you with the tools and techniques to present your chosen facts in a convincing and engaging manner.

The Resume Handbook will help you *win the interview*.

The rest is up to you!

Introduction

After reading many thousands of resumes throughout our careers, a single, recurring impression looms large and dominant in our minds: *Too many resumes are poorly written and the overwhelming majority of resumes are overwhelmingly dull!*

Ah, but a veritable work of "art vitae" does happen by on rare occasion, one illuminated with a spark of true, creative thought, and which is pleasing to the eye. Now, if this isn't of itself enough to make our lives exciting, it may at least be interesting to read, and maybe—just perhaps—it will inspire sufficient curiosity to invite the author in for a closer look, which is of course the purpose of a resume.

The purpose of this book is to increase the minute percentage of outstanding resumes, in case we have to read thousands more prior to retirement.

We have been careful to avoid the fat and wordy formats to which most books of this kind are prone. Instead, we've tried to heed our own advice on writing resumes by making our book interesting and to the point. *The Resume Handbook* presents the essential ingredients that go into successful resumes, with lucid explanations and the clearest of examples.

You can read through this book in less time than it takes to write a resume, then use it as a reference source when you are ready to begin writing your very own.

We've included examples of "The Best Resumes We've Ever Seen." You will quickly learn what makes them so effective, and how to apply their winning techniques to your own purposes. The chapter, "The Five Worst Resumes We've Ever Seen," illustrates some of the pitfalls to be avoided at all costs, and may prove equally instructive.

The Resume Handbook focuses on three major objectives:

- *Organization:* How to structure and give visual impact to your resume so it immediately captures the reader's attention.

- *The Basic Principles:* What to include and what to leave out of your resume, to avoid wasting the reader's time and running the risk of turning him or her off.

- *Accomplishments:* How to write action-oriented accomplishments by using action verbs, enabling you to represent yourself as a highly motivated achiever.

You'll also find sections on networking, using the Internet, cover and personal sales letters, and other helpful topics. However, our emphasis remains on writing resumes that will enable you to present yourself in the most appealing and engaging manner possible, to help you win the interviews you want.

—Art Rosenberg and Dave Hizer

A Message from the Authors

Since the original edition of *The Resume Handbook* was published in 1985, over 240,000 copies have been sold. The feedback we've received suggests that the reasons for our book's success lie in its clearly written style, direct and practical advice, and an occasional touch of humor. For a helpful book need not be dull and lifeless, any more than a winning resume.

Years of experience have convinced us that this new edition of *The Resume Handbook* will significantly help your job search in these troubled economic times. We are certainly interested in your feedback and invite you to contact us at *art.rosenberg@att.net*.

CHAPTER ONE
Looking for a New Job

Nearly everyone looks for a job during his or her lifetime. According to the U.S. Bureau of Labor Statistics, the average American worker does so every 3.6 years, and the National Bureau of Economic Research tells us that the average Jane and Joe work for ten different employers during their respective lifetimes. Given the increased volatility in the job market, we need to be ready for an accelerated rate of change.

Over 50 million North Americans are currently involved in some sort of career change or transition. More than one-third are currently employed. This is due in a large part to economic uncertainty, job and career dissatisfaction, fierce competition in the job market, and an increased awareness of alternative career opportunities.

These statistics are partially skewed, for there are firms that hire nearly as many new workers in a given year as their total number of employees. For example, a construction company with 100 workers may have to hire as many as 200 per year, due to enormous turnover. And service firms with as few as twenty-five full-time employees often need to hire four times that number each year in order to maintain a stable staff.

The bottom line is that if you're looking for a job, you are in excellent company. To compete successfully, you need a system that will give you an advantage. This is where *The Resume Handbook* can help. For whatever job search methods you may use, you'd better have a darned good resume to penetrate the screening processes used by most employers.

All They Know of You

The purpose of your resume is to get you invited for an interview. It precedes you in your job search like an emissary of goodwill, an advertisement of your skills, experience, and knowledge presented in their most favorable light. Until you meet the interviewer (if you ever do), the resume is *all* they know of you. Approximately one interview is granted for every 250 resumes received. Obviously, a mediocre resume will rarely win an interview and a poor one hasn't got a chance!

Research tells us that a piece of advertising matter has about 1½ seconds in which to attract the reader's interest. Someone sitting with a stack of 250 resumes (more likely a whole lot more) is simply unable to grant them equal time. Your objective is to position yours to receive its fair share of the interviewer's attention.

Read on . . . we'll show you how.

Who Needs a Resume?

You do—even if you're not looking for a job.

Fact: The majority of desirable positions are offered to individuals who are employed and who aren't necessarily seeking a new job. You never know when opportunity will knock, when the "job of a lifetime" may dangle within reach. Thus why it always pays to have an updated copy of your resume on hand for unexpected opportunities.

Fact: It is a valuable experience to observe your own career on paper. Your resume can place your past experience, growth, and goals into perspective, and help chart the path of your career's future.

Fact: Having a resume may help protect you from the unexpected, such as losing your job in an economic downturn. A well-prepared resume takes some of the anxiety out of the job search. This is especially true for the experienced professional who suddenly finds him- or herself competing for jobs against young professionals who may be better versed in the latest job-hunting techniques.

Resume Organization

There are three commonly used resume formats (examples in Chapter 4):

- *Chronological* resumes are safe for people with unbroken records of employment. This is a straightforward, easy-to-follow format that includes the dates of current and past employers.

- *Functional* (thematic) resumes focus on accomplishments rather than dates. This format is practical for those individuals with employment gaps due to unemployment or other activities they might prefer not to reveal (such as jobs from which they were fired or left after a short time, unsuccessful self-employment, prison terms, and a host of other reasons). It is also a better way to emphasize certain aspects of your career.

  Example: If you spent eleven years teaching engineering and only two years as an industrial engineer, a chronological resume would draw attention to your teaching background. But if you happened to be looking for an engineering position within a corporation, the functional format would allow you to play up your industrial experience and de-emphasize the academic side.

  People without very much experience may want to choose the functional approach. This tends to be the case with recent graduates and those seeking new (or planning to resume) careers after prolonged periods at home.

- *Combined* chronological/functional resumes can, under the right circumstances, combine the best of two worlds.

Resume Preparation

Regardless of which resume format you choose, it's best to get your thoughts together in the form of a list or outline before you begin. Composing an initial autobiographical outline requires serious preparation and contemplation. Find a quiet spot (office, den, or dining room table) where you feel comfortable and undisturbed. Set aside a period of four to five hours and, if possible, turn off the phone.

Collect all the materials you will need, including:

- Pens, pencils, or PC—whichever you prefer to use
- A lined notepad (at least 8½" x 11")
- A good dictionary and thesaurus
- Records of your past employment, education, and related materials
- Copies of former job applications and correspondence, if available
- Descriptions of the jobs for which you plan to apply
- A copy of *The Resume Handbook*

Now that you're suitably equipped, you can begin to formulate your own *resume strategy*. Be careful to observe the basic principles of resume writing, which follow.

CHAPTER TWO
The Basic Principles of Resume Writing

Writing a successful resume is an art, with certain basic principles that should be kept in mind. The following suggestions have been formulated through long years of exposure to all sorts of resumes. Major deviations from these "rules" are at your own creative—and professional—risk.

Brief is usually better: Try to fit the entire resume on a single page (especially if you are just beginning your career), and don't exceed two pages. Nobody likes to read resumes that are too long, especially if the length is due to poor organization and wordiness. An exception to this rule is for consulting resumes, which may need to list a variety of technical skills, projects, and clients comprehensively (for more information, please see Chapter 4).

Format: Your name (in bold type or in capital letters), address, and both home and work telephone numbers belong on top. Next come your objectives (if included) and a summary of your qualifications, accomplishments, employment history, education, and related activities and affiliations. Select a resume from the samples provided in Chapter 4 that most closely meets your needs and suits your style and use it as a model, or combine elements from several of the examples.

Education may precede employment history in certain cases, especially if a recent graduate or technical degree is more closely related to the desired position than your employment history. Recent graduates, with little or no work experience, have little choice.

Optional categories: These may include career objectives, summary of qualifications, and personal details such as date of birth, marital status, military record, and health.

- ***Career objectives:*** We are opposed to including objectives on a resume unless they are clearly stated and consistent with your accomplishments and demonstrated skills.

    If you do choose to include this section, bear in mind the difference between *career* and *job* objectives. A *career* objective is a long-range plan that may or may not relate directly to the job for which you are applying. A *job* objective is specifically linked to the opening you wish to fill. To avoid confusion, consider using the term "objective" by itself, which would be appropriate for many situations. Here are some examples of objectives:

A programming position enabling me to apply my technical and marketing experience and knowledge to Web-based marketing solutions.

An elementary (grades 3–6) teaching position in special education.

The potential dangers of stating an objective are:

Restricting your job search to a narrow and limited arena.

Discovering at the interview that the employer has a need that is different from what you were considering, but one in which you may be qualified and interested (*if* you are invited for the interview).

Confusing or turning off the reader.

Avoid terms like "challenging" and "rewarding," which are self-serving and of little interest to most employers. *Their* challenge and reward is to hire employees who can help their company.

Remember, your objectives can be honed specifically to the job for which you are applying in your cover letter (Chapter 10).

Summary of qualifications: A detailed resume that includes a wealth of professional experience can employ this idea effectively. The summary may be inserted in addition to, or instead of, a *statement of objectives*; or the two can be combined into a *qualifications and objectives* section.

At its best, a summary will entice the reader to read further; at its worst, it has the opposite effect. A summary is most helpful if the applicant has had an extremely diversified background, including (for instance) teaching and industry (see Chapter 4). It can also be useful if the resume extends beyond a single page. An effective and well-written summary attracts the reader's eye, brings the essence of your resume into focus, and compels the reader to move on to the main details.

Personal data: If your personal details are conventional and straightforward, they may lend an air of respectability to your image. However, any nonessential information that you offer is more likely to work against you.

Let's face it: Prejudices exist toward single women, unmarried men over a certain age, and older job seekers. Your date of birth may only serve to persuade potential employers to believe that you are too young or too old for a given job before they've even met you. Omit *any* reference to health, unless your physical or mental condition would limit your ability to perform typical job functions.

On the other hand, a military record may be worth mentioning if it includes some sort of relevant job training or experience (for example, technical or organizational; see resume 13 in Chapter 4 for an example).

Leave out:

- Reasons for having left a job—They won't enhance your image, and you may create a negative impression.
- Former (or desired) salary—You need to know as much as possible about the job in order to avoid asking for too little or too much. Don't risk putting yourself out of the running before you've even begun.
- Hobbies and memberships in social, fraternal, or religious organizations—Potential employers don't need this information, and you never know what may turn them off.
- Reasons for *not* having served in the military.
- Any potentially negative information about you (unless unavoidable), such as prison terms, lost lawsuits, and handicaps that may affect your job performance.
- The label "Resume" or "Vitae"—If the briefest glance does not clearly identify your resume as such, the label will not help.

Visual impact: Use the same type style throughout your resume, and use bold, italics, or all caps for headings and emphasis. Do not send out photocopies; spend a few dollars to have your resume professionally printed or use a high-quality laser printer . . . the difference is well worth the cost.

Print your resume on quality paper. Stick with white or off-white. Make sure the resume is *perfect*. Errors, typos, stains, abbreviations (*etc., e.g., i.e.*), technical jargon, and hip slang or buzzwords are strictly taboo. Get your final draft critiqued and proofread by someone reliable.

Ensure integrity: Poorly written resumes often lack internal integrity, so be sure that yours is consistent. Your job or career objective (if you use one) must be supported by the accomplishments you list. If you are interested in a senior position with an advertising firm, then you should emphasize your accomplishments in management, business development, and in creative programs you've developed.

If you include a "Summary of Qualifications," it must represent in brief the rest of your resume. If not, you will confuse the reader. The bottom line here is that your resume provides separate—but interrelated—facts.

Employment history: When writing a chronological resume, strike a balance between job content and accomplishments; the latter should be emphasized (as we'll explain in the next chapter). List your current position first, working back chronologically. De-emphasize the jobs you held further back in time. Avoid verifiable exaggerations that may someday constitute grounds for dismissal, but do use action verbs and phrases to best present the facts to your advantage (see Chapter 3).

Here's an example of a balanced job history:

1989 to present	Flinthall Electronics, Dover, Ohio. Manager of product testing. Supervise testing group consisting of seven research engineers. Group's mission was to create methods to test performance, safety, and durability characteristics of projected products. While heading up this group: • Initiated testing methods that reduced annual budget of group by 29%. • Received award of excellence for innovations in testing by *American Society of Research Engineers*—1999. • Increased group efficiency as measured by time and quantity parameters by 35%. • Developed three patented testing procedures during last four years.

In this example, the first paragraph clarifies the job's content—what was supposed to be done. This introduction sets up and brings clarity to the accomplishments.

Organizations of which you are a member: You may safely list the groups that show achievement or professional standing, such as the National Association of Certified Public Accountants, or the Tool & Diemaker's Guild. You can also indicate your leadership abilities as an officer or official in a strictly uncontroversial association, like the PTA or Junior Achievement. But stay away from listing political, religious, and potentially controversial groups, because they simply don't belong on resumes.

Awards: Be sure to list awards that relate to the kind of job you're seeking, such as Pulitzer Prizes, Oscars, or honorary doctorates. Leave out references to having won the league bowling or karate championship. While these achievements may bolster your ego, they can create uncertain images in the mind of the interviewer. In addition, they have nothing to do with the task at hand—winning an interview.

With these basic resume strategy guidelines in mind, it's time now to focus on how to make *your* resume stand out from all the others.

CHAPTER THREE

Stating Your Accomplishments

The *manner* in which you state your accomplishments is no less important than the details themselves. Active, energetic phrases attract more of the reader's attention than do dull or passive words. *Created*, for example, sounds more interesting than *began*; *promoted*, *instituted*, and *produced* are much more attention-getting than *worked on*, *became*, or *finished*.

In many cases, the very first word you use to describe an accomplishment can make the difference between an impressive resume and one that's just ho-hum. It may also make the difference between its being read or "filed." So before presenting the mechanics of stating your accomplishments in their best possible light, let's pause to digest "Hizer's 57"—a list of action verbs that show you are an *action person*, the kind employers notice.

Action Verbs

Hizer's 57

achieved	directed	organized
administered	eliminated	planned
advanced	established	prepared
advised	evaluated	produced
analyzed	expanded	promoted
authored	focused	provided
automated	headed up	published
coached	identified	reduced
conceptualized	implemented	researched
conducted	improved	restructured
contained	increased	reversed
contracted	initiated	saved
controlled	innovated	scheduled
coordinated	instituted	solved
created	introduced	streamlined
cut	led	supervised
decreased	maintained	taught
designed	managed	trained
developed	negotiated	trimmed

This does not pretend to be the ultimate list of action verbs. They can, however, be applied to virtually any field or industry, actively demonstrating why your skills would be an asset to any employer.

Now that you're armed with these effective action verbs, it's time to turn them into action phrases that best describe your accomplishments.

Action Phrases

Dull resumes tend to contain a lot of statements and descriptions that appear to have been copied directly from corporate personnel files. This, of course, is poor resume strategy. A better tactic is to employ phrases stressing your accomplishments in such a way as to attract—and hold—the reader's attention.

An interview-winning resume contains a balance of job content and accomplishments. It also has attention-getting style. You may refer to this as flair, technique, or pizzazz . . . in *The Resume Handbook*, we call it *impact*.

To illustrate the point, here are some contrasting examples of statements often found in resumes. Those on the left are dull; in addition, they tell only half the story: what was done. The action phrases on the right, on the other hand, present a larger context in which to evaluate accomplishments more fully.

They are, indeed, more interesting to read, due in large measure to their effective use of action verbs.

Dull	With Impact
1. Raised level of sales above previous year.	1. Reversed negative sales trend; sales up 31% over prior year.
2. Started new employee programs that lowered turnover.	2. Created and implemented two new employee relations programs (flextime and job posting), resulting in a 33% reduction in turnover.
3. Handled bookings for elderly pop group.	3. Managed bookings, travel, and accommodations for sexagenarian sextet.
4. Housewife of household with six people for past seven years.	4. Managed and organized six-member household with annual budget of $65,000.
5. Marketed new travel plan to corporations, increasing sales $19 million.	5. Initiated new market concept of packaging travel to corporations for incentive programs, resulting in sales of $19 million (more than double expectations).
6. Worked for losing gubernatorial candidate for six months.	6. Organized and coordinated political campaign for leading gubernatorial candidate.
7. Opened new sales offices in two cities that broke quotas ahead of schedule.	7. Researched feasibility, then established two new sales offices; both operated above sales quotas within two years (six months ahead of schedule).
8. Hired and trained six new lion tamers since 2001. Only one serious casualty.	8. Recruited, trained, and motivated six new lion tamers since 2001; five continue to excel.
9. Lowered operating costs in my division by $650,000.	9. Initiated cost reducing plan in my division, resulting in 27% ($650,000) cost reduction with no negative effect on production capability.

Dull	With Impact
10. Put on training sessions for supervisors in corporation.	10. Conducted leadership training for forty-eight supervisory and management level staff members.
11. Increased sales and profitability despite lower budget.	11. Expanded market penetration sales by 14%, and profitability during a period of budgetary cut-backs.
12. Contributed to making group much more efficient.	12. Increased group efficiency as measured by time and quantity parameters by 35%.
13. Wrote ornithology procedures manual for museum.	13. Conceptualized and authored eighty-eight-page ornithology procedures manual for museum zoological research department.

In many of the preceding examples, you'll notice a relationship between the action verb used in the phrases with impact and a more complete and detailed description of accomplishments. This is because action verbs invite further questions—even as you reflect on your achievements and write your resume.

Focus on accomplishments that had a noticeable or measurable effect on some part of the place where you worked. Use the following list of questions to stimulate your recollection of what you accomplished.

1. Were you able to increase sales or productivity? Did you meet or exceed goals, quotas, or expectations?
2. Did you cut losses and save money? Did you retain a key account or client?
3. Did you identify and resolve important issues? Don't dismiss what you consider obvious; it may be meaningful to someone else.
4. Did you install a new system or procedure? Include an indication of timelines, cost consciousness, or quality results.
5. Have you re-engineered procedures? What were the results?
6. Did you demonstrate your willingness to be a team player?
7. Have you shown leadership skills? Show how and what resulted.
8. Have you trained others to meet or surpass expectations? What training techniques did you use?
9. Did you introduce any new services or products? What resulted?
10. Have you served as a coordinator, liaison, representative, or committee member in any capacity that made a difference? What difference did it make?
11. Have you demonstrated a willingness to assume extra responsibilities or work?
12. Have you accomplished anything that was considered difficult or impossible?
13. Can you show a record of consistency and reliability? (Example: completing projects on time.)
14. Have you ever cleaned up someone else's mess?

15. Have you performed independently without close supervision? What were the results?
16. Have you ever gone way out of your way to provide exceptional service to a client or customer? What happened as a result?
17. Has your work performance been recognized by a superior? Why? What did you do?
18. Have you ever been told by a peer, superior, supplier, or customer that you made an important difference? What was the result?
19. What was the most extraordinary, fulfilling, and professionally satisfying thing you've ever done? What resulted?

A careful blend of action verbs and specific accomplishments will get the interviewer's attention. It may motivate him or her to call you in for a serious interview.

Take a look at the following examples and think about your own accomplishments:

- *Successfully managed,* for past eleven years, a five-member household with an annual budget of $59,200, while completing Associate of Business degree at Clinton Valley Community College.
- *Researched, wrote, and published* information booklet for graduating college seniors: "Don't Pass Go, Don't Collect Up to $200,000 Now."
- *Conceptualized and founded* Meadow Lane Day Care Center, which now cares for twenty-nine children daily.
- *Controlled* expenses on "Parents March for M.S."; treasurer for Imperial and Essex Counties.
- *Organized* food cooperative that purchased $119,000 in consumables during 2001.
- *Created* children's T-shirt design, then implemented marketing program resulting in gross sales in excess of $70,000.
- *Maintained* 3.9 grade-point average in business courses at Ohio State University. Completed eleven courses to date.
- *Elected* to represent Nevada State University at the International Congress on Energy Alternatives in Prague.
- *Chosen* over thirty-seven other trainees by senior management as member of four-person management trainee group organized to rewrite the training program we had just taken.
- *Created* neighborhood theater ensemble which, over the last nine years, has developed into the nationally renowned "Westgate Orchards Theatre Ensemble."
- *Written up in Oregon's Eye O-U* (alumni newspaper) as one of ten most promising freshmen in 2001.
- *Initiated* and headed ninety-member "Students for Intellectual Expansion"—University of Missouri's answer to president's challenge to create alternative energy.

- *Conducted* sensitive quality control study for Southeast Michigan Water Authority—written up in Michigan Congressional Record, June 2000, "Standing Ovation for H2O."
- *Formed* local Junior Chamber of Commerce, which has grown from nineteen to 291 members.
- *Elected* to Board of Directors of the $36 million asset Tri-County Employees Credit Union.
- *Originated* and published *Salescall*, an informational newsletter distributed to 144 sales representatives throughout the U.S. *Salescall* covers sales techniques, product knowledge, legislative updates, notes of competition, and technical changes.
- *Headed up* procedures group that eliminated nineteen obsolete reports and modified, or combined, fourteen others (out of a total of forty-nine) without reducing operational effectiveness.
- *Designed* assembly pivot arm that increased overall line speed by 9%, resulting in an increase in daily production of thirty-nine units (15% increase).
- *Produced* videotape program entitled "Here to Help," outlining Marcot's product servicing capabilities to current and prospective clients.
- *Instituted* self-developed safety program within my production wing of 179 employees, resulting in lost workday savings of 39% over previous three years.

The preceding accomplishment statements are action-oriented because they start with action verbs; the statements are achievement-oriented in that they demonstrate the writer's capability of organizing, completing, leading, and doing. They accomplish this by:

Using quantitative measures to emphasize to what extent the writer completed that achievement.

Example: Scored in the 95th percentile on seven out of the eight parts of the state licensing exam for electricians.

Using position to indicate the relative importance of the achievement.

Example: Awarded second place out of sixty entrants in the National Collegiate Debate Association "Debate 2002" in St. Louis.

Using action verbs to indicate selection over others.

Example: Selected fifth for the presupervisory awareness program at Big Sky Electric out of 195 candidates.

Using action verbs to indicate leadership in creating, initiating, or heading an activity of a group.

Example: Organized and was first chairperson of Moravia Valley Glass and Can Reclamation Center, which collected 119 tons of recyclable glass and aluminum during 2001. Example: Organized and led 36-member church bazaar group that successfully raised $28,760 over a two-year period.

For Students and the Newly Graduated

A special note to students, new graduates, and those returning to work after a lengthy absence: Remember to look outside the work arena in developing your accomplishment statements. With limited or outdated work experience, you need to explore your personal experiences for ways to sell yourself to a potential employer.

1. Consider writing about your membership and leadership involvement in campus clubs and organizations. Avoid mentioning controversial or unsanctioned groups.

    Example: "Captained intramural coed softball team that won campus championship, 2003. Recruited, coached, and motivated fourteen players."

2. Look for an accomplishment statement in a term project or paper that you wrote. This is especially advantageous if it relates to your job objective or career interest.

    Example: "Researched and wrote twenty-one-page term paper, entitled "Which Niche Now," that listed the latest approaches in identifying and appealing to your product's market. (Received an 'A.')"

3. Form an accomplishment statement around a noteworthy comment made by a professor, instructor, or teacher that shows your creativity, insight, or hard work.

    Example: "Recognized verbally by organic chemistry professor who stated that I had 'natural research instincts' and I was 'bound for greater heights'."

4. Include accomplishment statements that show initiative and responsibility.

    Example: "Initiated, organized, and led almost entire dormitory population in preparing for Parents' Day–June 2002. Parents were overwhelmingly united in their praise of the day's events."

5. Think in terms of specialized training and learning experiences that exhibit uniqueness or an interest in learning new things.

    Example: "Volunteered to stay after hours and without pay to learn and work with employer's bookkeeper in closing out the financial books; subsequently closed out next month's books on own—without pay."

For Those Returning to Work After an Absence

1. Include volunteer work—school, civil, or community.

    Example: "Selected by Lancaster County School Board as 'Volunteer of the Year,' 2003.

2. Identify how hobbies might provide material showing uniqueness or expertise.

    Example: "Featured in *Furniture Refinishing* magazine (April 2001) for volunteer work teaching high school sophomores and juniors furniture repair and refinishing."

3. Show how you have found ways to keep your skills updated.

    Example: "Established home-based research and advisory service using Internet resources to provide corporate clients with recent patent and copyright filings."

4. Explore how managing family issues can serve as work-relevant accomplishments.

    Example: "Conducted exhaustive research that led to identifying a rare learning disorder that doctors and clinicians had been unable to diagnose. Identification led to successful treatment and article in *Parents* magazine entitled 'How Parents Can Make a Difference.'"

5. Consider how continuing education (including self-development) shows your initiative and sense of responsibility.

    Example: "During 2000-2002 completed three Dale Carnegie courses on Sales, Leadership, and Public Speaking. Named top graduate in leadership program."

Describing Your Education

If your employment experience is limited, your educational background may be more relevant to the job you're seeking. In this case, your education will be the initial accomplishment you list. (See examples in the next chapter.) Regardless of whether it is your key accomplishment or subordinate to your job history, there are methods of presenting your educational background concisely and impressively.

For an individual with extensive employment experience, it is usually sufficient to list the bare details:

> 1999: B.S., Biology, Howard University, Washington, D.C.

> *or*

> Cornell University, Ithaca, N.Y.: M.B.A., Business Administration

You may, of course, list any academic honors earned:

> 2000: San Diego State University, San Diego, California: M.A., History *(cum laude)*.
>
> *or*

> University of New Hampshire, 2001: B.A. in Fine Arts; graduated *summa cum laude*.

If your employment experience is limited, it is a good idea to elaborate on educational achievements before employment:

> 2002—Bachelor of Arts Degree in Business Administration, University of Florida. Achieved 3.6 grade-point average (4.0 scale); specialized in management information systems. Senior project consisted of 223-page report on the compatibility of selected information retrieval systems. Excerpts were published in July 2001 edition of *M.I.S.*

> *or*

> Boston University, College of Communication, 2000. Maintained 3.5/4.0 GPA; emphasized newspaper journalism sequence. While in school, served as editor of *The Daily Free Press* (1998–2000); awarded John Scali Achievement Prize for best student investigative news story.

If you have extensive relevant work experience in an academic setting (as do researchers, law students, journalism students, and others), be sure to carefully describe your accomplishments with action phrases. Limited employment experience also necessitates creativity in describing other educational achievements. A lecture heard at college, work, or elsewhere may be described as:

> December 2001: Attended seminar on "Business Computer Languages" at RETI School of Electronics, Rapid City, SD.

> *or*

Summer 1998: Participated in week-long seminar on publishing procedures and marketing techniques, University of New Mexico.

List any relevant certificates you've earned:

Received "Fortran Programming Proficiency" certificate from ABC Business Institute, Phoenix, AZ: February, 1999.

or

Awarded certificate of proficiency in "Business Communication Machinery" from Control Info Institute, 1998.

If you lack a college degree, emphasize any classes attended or years completed. This can be worded so as to reflect that you're in the process of completing a degree:

UNIVERSITY OF MIAMI (Evening Division): B.S., Mathematics; in progress.

or

Currently working toward B.S. degree in Public Administration, University of Delaware.

People with a lot of professional experience commonly list the seminars, lectures, or certificate programs they have attended, and so should you. Those who haven't earned college degrees are advised to list their high school diplomas. For example:

Diploma (with honors), Davis High School, Mt. Vernon, N.Y.

or

Graduated (college preparatory courses) Edgewater High School, Orlando, FL.

All They Know of You

Following these guidelines on stating your accomplishments, your resume should fairly sing to an employer: *Call me in for an interview; I can help your company.* Remember, your resume is all they know of you until you walk through that door. The only way an employer can identify you as an action-oriented individual is from your resume, and action verbs will help you to accomplish this objective.

Having mastered the art of using action verbs, your remaining task is a mechanical one: plugging these action phrases into the following general format.

When stating your accomplishments, be sure to include:

- Name and location of the organization (city/state only; street address is unnecessary)
- Specific job title
- Job description
- Skills applied
- Skills acquired (if applicable)
- Significant accomplishments
- Dates of employment (unless using functional format)

In listing former jobs, it is recommended that you go back no more than eight to ten years, unless you've spent all that time with the same company or have something significant to list.

Gaps in employment dates of more than a month or two can be "hidden" (or briefly explained, e.g., sabbatical to complete degree, illness, military service, etc.) by extending dates of earlier and later employment, or even better, by employing a functional format.

Once you've stated your accomplishments using action verbs and phrases that embellish your performance, you've completed the most difficult part of writing an effective resume.

Ready to begin? Before you do, we suggest you take a look at Chapters Four and Five, to see how others have created their masterpieces . . . and disasters.

CHAPTER FOUR
The Best Resumes We've Ever Seen

The following resumes, which we have edited and modified, are among the best we've seen. They were selected from among the thousands we have reviewed in recent years to represent the various techniques and purposes we would like to share with you.

Each resume addresses a specific challenge and approach. You may find one that appeals to you; alternatively, you can draw upon elements from two or more to meet your personal needs.

The resumes are labeled as chronological (with dates), functional (thematic, without dates), and combined (both). They are organized according to the needs and objectives of different job seekers. Category examples:

- Limited experience
- Re-entering the workplace
- Secretarial
- Professional and managerial
- Technical
- Finance
- Sales and marketing
- Research and academia
- Executive level
- Senior
- Consulting
- Other

Of course, there is unavoidable overlap between some of these categories, e.g., professional and finance, technical, research and consulting, and so on. Still, we believe this organization will help our readers to find what they are looking for more easily and conveniently.

Resume Example #1: Limited Experience
A recent graduate shows an impressive list of achievements.

Hugo Lightly   22 Story Avenue

Lancaster, Pennsylvania 28717   (606) 555-1111

LIGHT ON WORK EXPERIENCE, HUGO LEADS OFF WITH HIS COLLEGE DEGREE

———— **EDUCATION** ————

B.A., Penn State University, August 2001
    Communications (emphasis on management), with additional major in Psychology.
    Junior and Senior GPA: 3.7: Overall GPA: 3.3

———— **SELECTED ACHIEVEMENTS** ————

- Scored in the *top three percent* of all graduating college seniors in the United States on the GMAT (GRADUATE MANAGEMENT ADMISSIONS TEST) and in the *top five percent* on the analytical/problem solving abilities portion of the GRE (GRADUATE RECORDS EXAMINATION).
- Elected by 104 residents to position as Hall President, Hershey Residence Hall, Penn State University, 1998-2001.
- Excellent writing ability as demonstrated by a 3.5 GPA in writing classes, 95% average on senior year term papers, and an entry in school creative writing annual.
- Chosen to be Research Assistant within School of Communications, Spring 1998 and as Teaching Assistant for Summer, 1999.
- Member of Dean's List at PSU three times (3.5 GPA).
- State Finalist in Radio Broadcasting two consecutive years.
- Excellent knowledge of Microsoft software.

EVEN LIMITED EXPERIENCE CAN BE PRESENTED PROFESSIONALLY.

———— **EXPERIENCE** ————

Penntec Research and Development, Inc.; Pittsburgh, Pennsylvania   2000–2001
Selected by Human Resources department manager to implement a Best Practices benchmarking survey and to assist in the writing and development of a corporation-wide employee training program for such areas as leadership, decision making, and communications. Solely responsible for the development of a 10-session leadership training program now in use throughout Penntec's North American operations.

The DH&S Group; Lancaster, Pennsylvania   2000–Present
Currently research associate doing marketing, product, and literature research for organizational development and team building consulting firm. Responsible for producing literature for the group and all word processing functions.

Kelly Temporary Services; Harrisburg, Pennsylvania   Intermittent
Offered permanent temporary position three weeks into temporary assignment at Kelly corporate headquarters. Assisted Accounts Receivables department manager in implementation of Total Quality Management program, and assisted Senior Account Specialist with Ford Motor, Philip Morris, and AT&T accounts.

Straits Diving; St. Ignace, Michigan   Summers, 1999 & 2000
Manager of a scuba diving operation with seasonal revenue of $250,000. Responsibilities included overall management of finances, retail sales, charter operation, purchasing, community relations, and dive instruction.

Combined

Resume Example #2: Transforming Skills
Transforming "housewifery" into job-related skills.

Lotta Toffer
327 Carmichael Avenue
Topeka, Kansas 66601
(913) 555-0000
E-mail: lotalots@aol.com

Objective

A challenging position that will both utilize and strengthen the organizational and motivational skills acquired in over eleven years of diverse, demanding responsibilities.

Experience

Recently completed over 11 years as a suburban homemaker and mother of three children, with success and skill in the following areas:

POSITIVE STATEMENT TRANSLATING WORK EXPERIENCE INTO JOB-RELATED SKILLS

- Budgeting - Accountable for the control and disbursement of an annual budget of $59,200.

- Prioritizing - Established schedules, met deadlines, and coordinated diverse tasks.

ACTION VERBS, IMPACT STATEMENTS

- Training and Supervision - Trained, instructed, and directed three junior associates, whose development was under my jurisdiction, in a wide variety of skills (from bicycle riding to writing term papers to managing a paper route).

- Recruitment, Interviewing, and Selection of Personnel - Hired a wide variety of professionals, including electricians, physicians, roofers, decorators, and baby-sitters.

- Purchasing - Analyzed and initiated purchases of low-budget to high-ticket items, including two automobiles, 950 square yards of carpeting, a twenty-four-cubic-foot freezer, swim club memberships, orthodontic and medical services, and six rooms of furniture.

VALIDATES CLAIM TO MANAGEMENT SKILLS

NOTE: All the above was accomplished successfully; during this time, a two-year Associate Degree was completed at Topeka Junior College, with membership on the Dean's list five out of six semesters.

NECESSARY IN THIS CASE

Excellent references available upon request.

Functional

Resume Example #3: Re-entering the Workplace
A homemaker with earlier professional experience pulls it all together.

Ramona Reentry

1404 Marlboro
Minneapolis, MN 55401

rree@mom.com
Home: (612) 555-1100

STRAIGHTFORWARD JOB OBJECTIVE

Objective

Journalism: Financial/Economics/General News Reporting

Significant
Accomplishments

CREATES THE IMPRESSION OF AN EFFICIENT
PERSON WHO GETS THINGS DONE

- Initiated, organized, and successfully led PTA.
- Sponsored one-year fund drive raising $86,250 (1995).
- Selected to five-member Emment County Scholastic Achievement Board, which distributes $150,000 in college scholarships to deserving, underprivileged high school seniors.
- Successfully organized 44-member petitioning group, which led to tax referendum being placed on Emment County election ballot (1999).
- Author of fifty-eight page book "Making Your Money Grow" directed at eight to sixteen year olds. Used in twenty-nine school districts.
- Wrote and co-directed play entitled "Life—A Contact Sport" about interpersonal skills useful for high school aged students.
- Chosen as one of four finalists for "Volunteer Citizen of the Year" (1999).
- Regular contributor to the *National Scholastic Achiever*, a quarterly journal. Have published eleven articles from 1993 to present. NOTEWORTHY

Education

DEMONSTRATES
ACTIVE INTERESTS

- B.S., Journalism: University of Chicago, 1993. 3.4/4.0 GPA; graduated "with distinction."
- Post-graduate study: Illinois State University, 1997–1999. Economics and Finance—8 classes at senior undergraduate level. 3.9/4.0 GPA.

Professional
Experience

National Scholastic Achiever   1999–Present

Part-time (twenty hours a week) position—research, writing, and office management.

Chicago Tribune   1993–1995
Special Events Reporter. Left voluntarily to raise family.

REFERENCES ARE IMPORTANT
FOR SOMEONE NOT RECENTLY
EMPLOYED

Excellent references available upon request.

Combined

Resume Example #4: Secretarial
An administrative professional with solid office skills and a record of steady employment.

Francis L. Workday

1404 Moore Avenue
Lincoln, MO 65338

Home: (417) 555-4771
flw22@aol.com

| CLEAN, DESCRIPTIVE, AND HELPFUL TO POTENTIAL EMPLOYERS |

Professional Summary

Administrative office professional with eleven years of progressively more challenging assignments. Strong computer skills in applications including word processing, spreadsheets, database, graphics, and accounting. Capable of rapidly learning new assignments involving decision making, organization of data, customer service, working cross-functionally with others and prioritizing responsibilities. Responsible and reliable; work quickly and accurately.

Technical/Office Skills

Software   Microsoft Office (Word, Excel, PowerPoint, Access); Lotus Notes. Able to adapt and learn any new software.

| A POSITIVE ATTITUDE IS ALWAYS APPEALING |

Work History

| A PROGRESSION OF DUTIES AND RESPONSIBILITIES |

1998 to Present   Union Carbide; Lincoln, Nebraska
Secretary and Administrative Assistant to Vice President in Charge of Sales.
Duties include: Preparing sales reports and basic market research reports; scheduling travel arrangements for nine sales professionals; supervise two other clerical assistants; insure that all filing, letters and reports produced by department meet quality standards for timeliness, clarity, and accuracy.

1993 to 1998   Hanson, Markham & Robb; Lincoln, Nebraska
Senior Secretary to Managing Partners of a seventeen-partner CPA firm.
Duties included: Overseeing all internal accounting for hours worked and billed. Supervising one other clerical assistant. Preparing minutes for all weekly partner meetings. Maintaining partner business development reporting and tracking. Maintaining all personnel files for firm's 29 employees. Recruiting and hiring all clerical/administrative personnel.

1991 to 1993   Second National Bank; Lincoln, Nebraska
Secretary, Commercial Loan Department
Duties included: Typing of all loan documents and departmental correspondence. Maintaining Loan Committee notes. Greeting and directing all guests.

Education and Training

Evelyn Steel Secretarial School, Lincoln, Nebraska   Received diploma and Top Student Award for eighteen-month program. 1995

Xerox Training Center, St. Louis, Missouri   Certificate of proficiency for Basic PC training. 1995

Personal

Enjoy travel, willing to relocate. | THIS CAN'T HURT |

Chronological

Resume Example #5: Sales and Marketing
Fast-track creative type seeking career enhancement.

Rita L. Fantasia   ritafan@yahoo.com

90 Treefilled Lane   Phone: Home (503) 555-5252
Hillsboro, Oregon 97123   Office (503) 555-2525

Employment

Venus Beauty Products, Portland, Oregon   1998–Present
Major beauty products supply distributor and retailer, annual sales of $30 million.
Proprietary Market Manager
Responsibilities: SIGNIFICANT RESPONSIBILITIES
• Buyer of 40 proprietary line items for 38 distribution centers nationwide.
• Annual open to buy budget: $8 million.
• Product and package planning, design, and development.
• Market analysis and research.
• Sales forecasting and evaluation of new and existing products.

Achievements: ACTION STATEMENTS REVEAL THE FULL RANGE OF
                         ACCOMPLISHMENTS IN A MEANINGFUL CONTEXT
• Established annual budget for new product development.
• Initiated seven new products from planning to point of purchase within ten months.
• Designed and authored a training manual for sales staff.
• Presented several slide presentations for training sessions.

Devon Incorporated, New York, New York   1991–1997
Account Manager
Responsibilities:
• Sales of cosmetic line through three levels of distribution: manufacturer to distributor, retailer, and
  consumer.
• Traveled 34 states with average annual sales of $2.3 million.   SPECIFIC FIGURES ENHANCE CREDIBILITY
• Conducted sales training meetings, seminars, and workshops for distributors and retailers.
• Created and designed displays, exhibits, and promotional materials for trade shows.

Achievements:
• Selected by Devon administrators to open select new markets with distributors and retailers in 22
  states.
• Designed, complete with layout and copy, photo-ready "Devon Advertising."
• Implemented new product promotion, including product, display, and promotional material.

Awards:
• Devon Sales of the Month Award (19 times).
• Best Sales Presentation Award (1994, 1996, 1999).   THE TYPES OF AWARDS THAT GET ATTENTION

Education

1990 Oregon College, Medford, Oregon: BS, Fashion Merchandising and Marketing.

Foreign Languages: French.   SOLID ACADEMIC CREDENTIALS

Chronological

Resume Example #6: Sales and Marketing
An administrator planning a career change.

ELLEN McSELLWELL

310 El Camino Road
San Diego, California 92103

Residence: (619)555-0000
Business: (619)555-0001
sellme@blah.com

OBJECTIVE   HOSPITAL AND MEDICAL SALES REQUIRING EXTENSIVE EXPERIENCE WITH STATE-OF-THE-ART MEDICAL EQUIPMENT, OUTSTANDING COMMUNICATIONS SKILLS, AND STRONG MOTIVATION.

> PARTICULARLY IMPORTANT TO STATE OBJECTIVE WHEN CHANGING CAREERS

PROFESSIONAL ACCOMPLISHMENTS

> CLEVER AND COMPETITIVE

- Successfully conducted training seminars for nearly two hundred supervisory personnel in interpersonal skills.

- Developed reputation for simultaneously coordinating numerous involved projects. Written up in *Hospital Administrator* magazine, 1998.

- Retained by three directors. Appointed to current position over fourteen other qualified candidates.

- Achievement-motivated, conscientious, objectives-directed. Obtained highest performance rating for three years.

> SALES-ORIENTED

- Adept at problem resolution and public relations. Regularly represent hospital at major civic gatherings.

- Experienced in the development of management systems, including the administration of a $4.3 million budget.

- Active member of Medical Equipment Review Committee, 1999-2001.

- Received U.S. security clearance.

EMPLOYMENT HISTORY

1998 - Present: Administrative Assistant to the Director, San Diego Memorial Hospital
1992 - 1998: Administrator to the Chief of Medical Administration, San Diego
1990 - 1992: Sold LaBelle health and beauty products door-to-door in West Virginia

EDUCATION   B.A., Administrative Management, 1990
Marshall University; Huntington, West Virginia

Additional course work at University of San Diego in Group Dynamics, Management, and Psychology

ADDITIONAL EDUCATION

> UTILIZING SKILLS AND ACCOMPLISHMENTS TO CONSTRUCT A NEW CAREER

Advance Management   Hospital Supervision
AMA Supervisory Skills   Kepner-Tregoe Problem Solving

PERSONAL   Able and willing to relocate and/or travel extensively.

> KEY STATEMENT FOR ANYONE WANTING TO BREAK INTO SALES

Combined

Resume Example #7: Sales and Marketing
An upbeat, creative presentation of an impressive track record in big-ticket marketing.

Merrie R. Noël
200 Nesbit Trail
Alpharetta, Georgia 30201
(404)555-0000
yuletime@atp.com

OBJECTIVE   Endless horizons in marketing or sales management with a progressive, dynamic company that needs and appreciates a results-oriented and highly experienced professional.

PROFESSIONAL ACHIEVEMENTS

STRATEGIC ACCOUNT MANAGER
- Achieved superior track record in developing new business.
- Implemented new market strategies to establish added value programs resulting in $17 million of new business over a two-year period.
- Researched and analyzed market trends in specific consumer and industrial market segments to ensure fitness of products for growth.

RESULTS THAT COUNT

SENIOR FIELD MARKET DEVELOPMENT SPECIALIST
- Identified and developed over $10 million of new business.
- Developed successful partnerships with strategic end user companies.

LONG- AND SHORT-TERM SUCCESSES

- Positioned new materials for developing applications providing manufacturing advantages to the end user.
- Integrated resources into end user engineering and design functions to optimize material selection, performance, and design for manufacturability.
- Coordinated product, molding, and design seminars resulting in joint development programs with end user companies.

VICE PRESIDENT

ENTREPRENEURSHIP

- Co-founded First Source Corporation, a manufacturer and distributor of specialty and proprietary chemicals for the food, pharmaceutical, and personal care industries.
- Nurtured this entrepreneurial venture from infancy into a $3 million business in thirty-six months.
- Maintained responsibility for sales, marketing, profit, and loss.

PRODUCT MANAGER, SILICONE FLUIDS   MORE SOLID RESULTS
- Developed and implemented marketing strategies for nationally marketed silicones.
- Increased sales volume from $7 million to $12 million by second year.
- Motivated, directed, and routed activities of seven sales representatives and twenty-two distributors.
- Designed, coordinated, and implemented a professional/educational training program for corporate and distributor sales forces.

Combined

SALES REPRESENTATIVE, INORGANIC CHEMICALS
- Conducted extensive market research project on fire extinguishing agent. Study resulted in $2 million gross sales within eleven months of completion.
- Increased department's sales from $10 million to $13 million after twelve months.

ASSISTANT TO DIRECTOR OF MARKETING
- Coordinated product evaluations/approvals with major U.S. customers for the eight products sold to U.S. licensees abroad.
- Conducted extensive market research projects to assist in developing product strategies for U.S. market.

BUYER, IMPORT PURCHASING
- Directly responsible for purchasing $75 million of products (raw material ingredients and imported resale items).

EMPLOYMENT HISTORY

HF PLASTICS, Pittsfield, Massachusetts	**1993 TO Present**
STRATEGIC ACCOUNT MANAGER	1996 - Present
SENIOR FIELD MARKET DEVELOPMENT SPECIALIST	1994 - 1996
FIELD MARKET DEVELOPMENT SPECIALIST	1993 - 1994
FIRST SOURCE CORPORATION, Cedar Hills, Illinois	**1987 TO 1993**
VICE PRESIDENT	1991 - 1993
POUNE-ROLANC, INC., Tillamook Junction, New Jersey	**1982 TO 1991**
PRODUCT MANAGER, SILICONE FLUIDS	1987 - 1991
SALES REPRESENTATIVE, INORGANIC CHEMICALS	1986 - 1987
ASSISTANT TO DIRECTOR OF MARKETING, ORGANIC CHEMICALS	1984 - 1986
BUYER, IMPORT PURCHASING	1982 - 1984

EDUCATION

B.A.–Education, French: University of Delaware, 1974

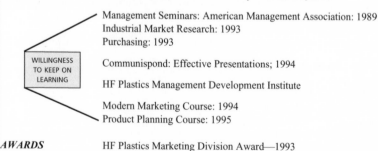

Management Seminars: American Management Association: 1989
Industrial Market Research: 1993
Purchasing: 1993

WILLINGNESS TO KEEP ON LEARNING

Communispond: Effective Presentations; 1994

HF Plastics Management Development Institute

Modern Marketing Course: 1994
Product Planning Course: 1995

AWARDS

HF Plastics Marketing Division Award—1993
HF Plastics Marketing Division Award—1994

Resume Example #8: Product Development
A highly experienced, versatile, professional manager who puts his best foot forward.

Christopher Libidos
Email: christoslib@abc.com

42 East 73rd Avenue
Tulsa, OK 74115

Home: 405/555-0000
Office: 405/555-0001

ABILITY TO IDENTIFY, FORMULATE, and MARKET HIGH PAYOFF PROJECTS: Developed projects that led to birth of 6,000 terminal communications network, $40 million-a-year wholesale company (the Arbor House Specials seen on TV), installing M.B.O., annual marketing plan in division of 1450, and an accounting system for bookstores.

> WELL-PHRASED HEADINGS

ABILITY TO START, GROW, AND MANAGE DEPARTMENTS: Started and managed: 5 training departments, research department, personnel department, and district sales office. Played key role starting 70 national account sales departments and 2 research departments.

P&L RESPONSIBILITY: Started division with $166,500 budget; now over $4.8 million.

> IMPRESSIVE NUMBERS

ABILITY TO WORK AT TOP LEVELS: Setting up board summit meetings to develop corporate objectives. Directly responsible to board for several projects. Staff person in charge of FOUR board committees. Serviced group coverage working with top management and unions.

SCOPE OF TRAINING EXPERIENCE: Managing and delivering: Sales training, management and organizational development, plus clerical and technical training. Developing, staffing, and selling 50 workshops with 5,000 enrollees per year, throughout North America.

SCOPE OF RESEARCH EXPERIENCE: Managing: Market research, new product development, operations improvement, R&D, and fact base development and maintenance. Create and conduct census of retail flower shops, primary source of data for floral industry.

Positions:

> COMBINATION OF EXPERIENCES SHOWS VERSATILITY

1997–Present	Director, Education and Research Division. Arbor House. International association; 1200 retail bookstores.
1994–1997	Management Consultant for consulting firm of Martell and Coxwell, Inc. Worked with National Association of Healthcare Affiliates, Timon Mufflers, and Oceanic Airlines.
1992–1994	Manager, Employee Development Department, Ohio Healthcare Affiliates.
1987–1992	Manager of various sales, training, and personnel functions. Including the Automobile Club of Ohio.

> EMPHASIS ON CONTINUING EDUCATION

Education: BA, Economics, Washington State University, Seattle, Washington. Over 1500 classroom hours at University of Tulsa.

> NOTICE THE AMOUNT OF IMPACT A ONE-PAGE RESUME CAN EVOKE!

Combined

Resume Example #9: Product Development
Career enhancement on the middle-management level.

Marvin R. Upbound

12 Arcadia Drive
El Paso, Texas 79901

upbound@yahoo.com
Telephone: (512) 555-6543 (Res.)
(512) 555-1111 (Bus.)

| SPECIFIC AND AMBITIOUS |

Career Objective

To direct a dynamic, ambitious (small or medium-sized) electronics corporation, and to help it grow into a major industry player.

**Employment
1993 to Present**

| GOOD BALANCE BETWEEN HISTORY AND ACCOMPLISHMENTS |

P. Reynolds Corporation, El Paso, Texas—*Director of Research and Development. Responsible for new product development and testing from innovation through feasibility. Includes management of a staff of twenty-three.*

- *Recruited* and developed research team of twelve engineers within eighteen months on job. No turnover on staff to date.

| MEASURABLE SAVINGS |

- *Developed* methodology of counter redesign of electronic sensing devices. This saved corporation $400,000 in first year of implementation.
- *Managed* R&D team responsible for major design changes to production facility resulting in 30% labor savings.
- *Led* research team that designed and rolled out Lithium Sulfate Battery that tripled mileage capability of electric automobile.

1986 to 1993

Laboratory Testing Corporation, Little Rock, Arkansas—*Senior Research Supervisor. Headed up eight-person product testing group responsible for establishing performance specifications.*

- *Initiated* group performance standards that allowed for "on-time" completion standard of 92%. Prior group had maintained 55% standard.

| QUANTIFIABLE RESULTS |

- *Created* test procedures that revealed product design errors, saving client manufacturers over $2 million during four years in this position.

Research Analyst. Member of a new tooling group developing and testing newly installed manufacturing lines involving high-usage, electronically-controlled feeder and assembly units.

- *Supervised* four-person group that blueprinted wiring schematics for entire final production assembly line for Volkswagen of America.

| SHOWS INITIATIVE |

Used computer line tracking design of our own making (first time used within automotive industry).
- *Promoted* to group supervisor (youngest supervisor of research group in corporation).

Education

University of Texas at El Paso, BS and MSEE 1986. Completed graduate work with a 4.8 GPA out of possible 5.0.

Awards

American Society of Electrical Engineers—"Research Engineer of the Year," 1991. Received recognition for usage of voltage conductors in high-use assembly units.

| A RELEVANT REWARD |

Chronological

Resume Example #10: Health Care
A health care professional with hands-on technical skills and extensive experience.

Mary Salvas-Mladek, CRA, CST, COA

6 Westcliff Drive   home: 516 473-9584
Mt. Sinai, NY 11766   work: 516 444-4099

> THE POINT OF THIS OBJECTIVE IS TO EXPLORE A NEW CAREER PATH IN SALES

OBJECTIVE   To apply my twenty three years of experience in ophthalmology, and
                            my personal acquaintance with the ophthalmological community—
                            particularly in Long Island—to effective pharmaceutical sales
                            representation.

PROFESSIONAL ACCOMPLISHMENTS

Department of Ophthalmology, SUNY @ Stony Brook   Stony Brook, New York
Outpatient Clinic Supervisor   1990–Present
Supervise five technicians and five administrative staff in daily support of seven staff
ophthalmologists and two residents. Maintain regular personal contact with area ophthalmologists to
facilitate appropriate service referrals.
Senior Retinal Photographer and Ophthalmic Technician   1984–1990

Retina Consultants of Michigan   Southfield, Michigan
Senior Retinal Photographer, First Surgical Assistant, Ophthalmic Technician   1983–1984
Obertynski Eye Care Center   Dearborn, Michigan
Retinal Photographer, First Surgical Assistant, Ophthalmic Assistant   1983–1984
Arnold Turtz, MD, Lawrence Yannuzzi, MD, Yale Fisher, MD   New York, NY
Ophthalmic Technician   1976–1977
Johns Hopkins Hospital—Wilmer Institute   Baltimore, Maryland
Ophthalmic Technician   1972–1974

EDUCATION   > IN THIS PROFESSION, EDUCATION IS AN ONGOING REQUIREMENT
[Maintain minimum of twenty-five continuing education credits annually.]

Marygrove College   Detroit, Michigan
National Certification as Surgical Technologist.

Eastern Connecticut State University   Willimantic, Connecticut
BA, History and Secondary Education.

Woodstock Academy   Woodstock, Connecticut
Academic Diploma.

RELATED PROFESSIONAL ACTIVITIES   > DIRECTLY RELEVANT TO HER PROFESSION

Certified Retinal Angiographer; Certified Technologist; Certified Ophthalmic Assistant
Member, Ophthalmic Photographer Society since 1978 [Vice President, L.I. Chapter O.P.S.]
Member, Association of Surgical Technologists since 1979 [past Chapter President]
Member, Joint Commission Allied Health Personnel

Chronological

Resume Example #11: Professional
An engineer with well-chosen accomplishment statements and a marketing flair.

Julio Iglesias Garcia

1001 ASUNCION
SAN JUAN, PR 00920

TEL.: 807/555-2333
HOLA@PRI.COM

Employment
1998 to PRESENT

Carib Electro Corporation, San Juan—Service and Quality Control Manager. Responsible for field and customer service activities along with quality control inspection of equipment to insure compliance with customer, OSHA, and JIC standards. Additional responsibilities include purchasing and technical service manual writing.

ATTENTION: PROSPECTIVE
EMPLOYERS

- Organized six-person service department to perform SAE certification testing verification of systems, resulting in 60 increase in contract revenues, along with warranty and non-warranty repairs leading to a 45 increase in repeat sales.
- Wrote technical operation and maintenance manuals for all systems manufactured.
- Reduced purchasing costs by 32 by developing and utilizing purchasing program for TRS80 computer. BOTTOM-LINE ORIENTED

1992 to 1998

ABZ Corporation, Xeroradiography Division—Technical Specialist. Responsible for field service and support of all technical representatives and contractors within designated region.

- *Promoted* from technical representative in Ponce branch to specialist within nine months of employment; became responsible for San Juan territory.
- *Reduced* nationwide service call rate by developing and implementing various in-field system retrofits.
- *Relocated* to develop new area in Denver-based territory, resulting in area sales increase of thirty-five systems the following year.

GETS RESULTS

Education

DRAWS OUT BUSINESS AND
HUMAN BEHAVIOR CLASSES

New York University, November 1992—Bachelor of Applied Science, Electronic Engineering Technology. Graduated with 3.95/4.0 GPA; primary concentrations in business communication, personnel administration, human resource management, business law, principles of marketing, and behavioral psychology.

RETS Electronic, June 1982—Associate's Degree in Electronic Engineering Technology. Second Class FCC Radio Telephone license.

Activities

Participating member of Society of Technical Communication (STC).

Special Skills

Bilingual (English/Spanish) ESSENTIAL FOR THIS LOCATION

Chronological

Resume Example #12: Professional
A research scientist who wants to keep his options open.

Eugene Chen

29 Vauxhall Road   Work: (317) 555-1587
Indianapolis, Indiana 46250   Home: (317) 555-9299

Employment History

• **WALLACE LABS, INDIANAPOLIS, INDIANA**   **1998–PRESENT**
Research Scientist
Research and coordinate development of enzyme immunoassays for diagnostic products.
Responsibilities include developing and implementing protein purification procedures, enzyme-
antibody conjugates, and solid phase technology for EIAs. Develop scaleup procedures to be used in
manufacturing diagnostic products. | CLEAR DESCRIPTION OF ACTIVITIES |

• **ACADEMIC PRESS, NEW YORK, NEW YORK**   **1992–1998**
Production/Project Editor
Coordinated production of scientific treatises and textbooks from manuscript to bound book.
Participated in planning of marketing strategies. Edited and rewrote technical material.

| VERY DIFFERENT FROM PREVIOUS PARAGRAPH |

• **AMERICAN INSTITUTE OF PHYSICS, NEW YORK, NEW YORK**   **1989–1995**
Production/Project Editor
Controlled production of *Review of Scientific Instruments*, a monthly journal. Rewrote and edited
technical manuscripts.

Education

• **INDIANA MEDICAL CENTER, INDIANA STATE UNIVERSITY, BLOOMINGTON, INDIANA**   **1994–1999**
Ph.D. in Pharmacology
Past five years have included extensive laboratory research and experimentation in the following areas:

Drug receptor studies   Drug-induced changes in enzyme activity
Regulation of in-vitro cell proliferation   Protein biochemistry
HPLC (attended seminar course)   Enzyme purification

• **UNIVERSITY OF ILLINOIS (DOWNSTATE), URBANA, ILLINOIS**   **1986–1990**
B.S. in Biology
Graduated summa cum laude; 3.81 cumulative index. Elected to several honor societies; received
Dean's Award for scholastic excellence. | WORTH MENTIONING |

Chronological

Publications   IMPORTANT FOR A RESEARCHER

- March 2001: *Biochemical Pharmacology* (Vol.34, No.6, pp. 811-819). Title: Effect of Streptozotocin on the Glutathione S-transfers of mouse liver cytosol.
- August 1999: *Journal of Laboratory and Clinical Medicine* (Vol.100, No.2, pp. 178-185). Title: Identification of a glucocorticoid receptor in the human leukemia cell line K562.
- November 1998: *Blood* (Vol.58, No.5, Suppl. 1, p. 120(a)). Abstract: same title as article above.

Related Activities

Downstate, University of Indiana: Instruction of medical students in pharmacology. Tutored undergraduate students in science and mathematics.

Resume Example #13: Professional
Leaving the military for a career in business.

Abel Baker

127 Hampton Street
Rockville, MD 20850

abcharlie@cap.org
Residence: (301) 555-3784
Answering Service: (301) 555-4895

Qualifications and Objectives

Rising from staff sergeant to the rank of captain is a clear indication of reliability, leadership, and character. Ten years of highly successful logistics management have prepared me to manage the transportation/trucking division of a medium-sized organization in need of cost efficiency and innovation. | POSITIVE AND CONVINCING |

Work Experience

- Organized, managed, and budgeted for a 140-vehicle transportation center with an annual operating budget of nearly $3 million.
- Initiated, developed, and directed a computer scheduling system that resulted in a 25% | COST SAVINGS | improvement of deliveries and an annual cost savings of $400,000.
- Created and implemented a revised bidding system on all vehicles purchased, allowing for quicker purchase decisions and increased opportunity for price reductions to multiple purchases. | EFFICIENCY |
- Effectively implemented personnel policies that led to a 19% increased efficiency rating over a two-year period. Received two commendations from management leadership.
- Improved measurement and communication of safety-related issues, resulting in nineteen months of accident-free work activity (one month short of the all-time division record). | CONCISE, BALANCED, COMPREHENSIVE STATEMENTS |

Work History

1996 - Present: Regional Director, Transportation and Logistics Command, U.S. Army, Washington, D.C.
1990 - 1996: Director, Transportation Section, Fort Campbell, Georgia | PROMOTED THROUGH THE RANKS |
1984 - 1990: Division Manager, Motor Pool, Fort Campbell, Georgia
1982 - 1984: Supply Officer, 3rd Army, Stuttgart, Germany

| ALWAYS LIST SUCCESSFUL MILITARY ACHIEVEMENTS |

Military Rank
Captain, U.S. Army

Education
Diploma, Greensboro High School, Greensboro, North Carolina

Foreign Languages
German

| EMPHASIZES SKILLS AND EXPERIENCE THAT ARE OF INTEREST TO POTENTIAL EMPLOYERS; DE-EMPHASIZES THOSE THAT ARE LESS SO |

Combined

Albert A. Torre   E-Mail: atorre@si.rr.com
63 Venus Lane   Business: 212-778-7657
Staten Island, N.Y. 10314   Residence: 718-494-7518

Profile: A highly motivated and effective business analyst experienced in project
management and software implementation. Specialties encompass financial,
institutional and retail applications. Proven strengths include problem solving,
system specifications development and system test coordination. Consistent
record of promotions and increased responsibilities over the past thirteen years
from programmer to project and business manager.

> A CLEAR AND INVITING
> SUMMARY OF EXPERIENCE
> AND ACCOMPLISHMENTS

Professional Experience:

Prudential Securities, Incorporated (PSI)

Assistant Vice President, Branch Automation   *1999–Present*
- Serve as facilitator between business units and systems areas to define and document
  project requirements.
- Develop business specifications and provide programmers with requirements for
  technical specifications.
- Create test plans and condition catalogs.
- Conduct user training and systems demonstrations.

> GROWTH AND RECOGNITION
> WITH THE SAME EMPLOYER

Project Lead, Securities Over The Wire System (SOW)   *1999–2001*
- Developed design for new system to allow branch office users to ship and track
  clients' physical securities being sent to the home office for re-registration,
  liquidation, redemption and related processes.
- Designed new GUI screens to replace existing CICS display utilizing Visual Basic
  and HTML.
- Implemented Branch to Home Office mainframe interface to replace Teletype
  functionality.
- Developed automated Document Requirement function, which performs a
  systematic notification to a branch of required documents for executing a SOW
  without home office consultation.

Senior Analyst, Average Price System & Trade Allocation
  and Correction System   *1998–2001*
- Collaborated with senior management to prioritize all Quality Assurance issues to
  satisfy user requirements and ensure timely software releases of new applications.
- Trained users on system functionality and coordinated test plan execution for
  Securities Database.
- Assisted developers with bug fixes, user testing, and acceptance testing.
- Reduced manual workload by 35% by automating Broker Order Entry and
  Correction systems.

Chronological

Albert A. Torre
___

Project Lead, Standing Instruction Database System (SID)   *1998–1999*
- Developed new system to automate the linking of PSI's institutional accounts to the Depository Trust Company's (DTC) database. This enabled Standing Instruction additions, deletions, and updates to be applied systematically.
- Collaborated with users to create an interface to systematically retrieve Standing Instructions from DTC and store them on PSI's database each time a new institutional account is created.

Business Analyst, Year 2000 Certification Project   *1997–1998*
- Performed testing on all institutional systems (DVP) to verify Year 2000 compliance.

Supervisor / Systems Analyst, Corporate Securities Systems Group   *1992–1997*
- Designed and implemented new Fraud Detection System to detect unusual client and employee activity which was being conducted for illegal or improper purposes.
- Developed Early Detection System to monitor debit card activity for Visa cards issued to PSI's COMMAND clients and alert investigators of potential fraudulent Visa activity.

Programmer, OCR / Data Entry Department   *1989–1991*
- Coded new applications for the Optical Character Recognition (OCR) System. This enabled handwritten new account documents to be read automatically by the system eliminating the manual data entry process.
- Designed New Accounts documents to be used within the OCR system.

Software skills: Microsoft Office, Microsoft Project, Visio, working knowledge of DB2, COBOL, and HTML

Education: B.B.A., Management Information Systems, Pace University, New York, NY, 1989

> APPROPRIATE SKILL-SETS AND ACADEMIC CREDENTIALS ROUND OUT THE PICTURE

Chronological

Resume Example #15: Professional
A hospital care specialist demonstrates his versatility and broad range of skills.

Robin Jection

1 Maywood Road
Roanoke, VA 24014

RJCARE@apple.com
Residence: (804) 555-0001
Business: (804) 555-1000

EXPERIENCE

October 1999 to
Present

MEDICAL CARE ASSOCIATES Asheville, North Carolina

GENERAL MANAGER

Directly responsible for all operations of a Medicare-certified home health care agency with annual revenue of $6,200,000. Major services include home health care, private duty care, and supplemental staffing. Nine hundred full- and part-time employees; five branch offices.

DEMONSTRATES ORIENTATION
AND VALUE OF
MANAGEMENT ACTION

- Reorganized internal operations, resulting in monthly savings of $16,000.
- Implemented marketing programs and internal controls that resulted in 20% increase in sales.
- Managed successful transition from franchise operation to corporate branch.
- Directed implementation of computerized client and employee information system.

March 1994 to
October 1999

WALTER A. CUMMINS HOSPITAL SYSTEM Mobile, Alabama

DIRECTOR OF MANAGEMENT SERVICES -
BEAUMONT SHARED SERVICES, INC.
November 1995 to October 1999

Responsible for several major components of $30,000,000 per year for-profit subsidiary of hospital. Responsibilities included contract management, management consulting, strategic planning, business development, and home health care.

QUANTIFIABLE
RESULTS

- Planned and implemented establishment of durable medical equipment subsidiary; generated over $400,000 in revenue. $40,000 in profit during first year.
- Initiated first comprehensive strategic planning process for Cummins Shared Services.
- Expanded contract management to include four hospitals and various consulting projects; generated revenue in excess of $200,000 per year.
- Designed comprehensive wage and benefit program for Shared Services employees; reduced personnel expenses by 15%, but maintained current staffing levels.
- Invited to speak as guest lecturer for Alabama Hospital Association on hospitals and home health care.

Chronological

Resume Example #15 continued

Robin Jection

> VERSATILE AND
> ADVENTURESOME

ASSISTANT DIRECTOR   *March 1994 to October 1995*
Complete administrative responsibility for patient support departments of 950-bed teaching hospital. Responsible for 520 employees and annual budget of $6,600,000.

- Planned and helped initiate conversion of former school into comprehensive outpatient health center.
- Organized and conducted major consulting projects in Nigeria and Saudi Arabia.
- Initiated the planning process required to streamline functions of patient service departments.

September 1992 to
March 1994

ARKANSAS COMMUNITY HOSPITAL   Little Rock, Arkansas
ADMINISTRATOR
Full responsibility for twenty-five-bed acute care hospital with annual budget of $2,500,000.

March 1980 to
March 1986

NORTH VIRGINIA HOSPITAL SYSTEM   Arlington, Virginia
ADMINISTRATIVE ASSOCIATE   *February 1991 to March 1992*
Responsible for management functions of Clinical Pathology Department, which employed 250. Areas of responsibility included: fiscal management, laboratory and employee representation to administration, operational policies and procedures.

PERSONNEL ASSISTANT   *November 1989 to January 1991*
Responsible for provision of personnel services to all areas of hospital. Developed department's data processing systems. Administered wage and salary and grievance programs.

FINANCIAL ANALYST   *March 1988 to October 1989*
Assisted in preparation of revenue, expense, and capital budgets. Prepared and analyzed monthly variance reports and financial statements. Managed hospital's investment portfolio.

MILITARY
SERVICE:

U.S. ARMY   *November 1984 to November 1986*
Stationed at Pentagon. Honorable discharge.

EDUCATION:

M.B.A.	**Howard University**	**1990**	**Hospital Administration**
M.A.	**Jackson State**	**1988**	**Guidance and Counseling**
B.S.	**Morgan State**	**1984**	**Economics and Business Administration**

AFFILIATIONS:

AMERICAN COLLEGE OF HOSPITAL ADMINISTRATORS (member)

Chronological

Resume Example #16: Professional
A graphic design professional tracks his progression into management.

Michael Angelo

3000 S. Valley View Blvd.
Las Vegas, Nevada 89102

cistine@aol.com
(702) 555-9999

OBJECTIVE

| WELL-STATED OBJECTIVE |

Management position in visual communications where strong operations management, graphic design capacity, and ability to develop staff will contribute to the productivity and profitability of the organization.

PROFESSIONAL SUMMARY

| OBJECTIVE SUMMARY BACKED BY DETAILS THAT FOLLOW |

Versatile graphic design professional with thirty years of marketing-oriented experience including production management, two- and three-dimensional graphic problem solving, staff development, logistic sensitivity, in-depth knowledge of reproduction systems, and long-standing record in creative resolution of customer needs.

SIGNIFICANT ACCOMPLISHMENTS

| SPECIFIC MEASURABLE ACCOMPLISHMENTS |

MANAGEMENT, OPERATIONS

- Restructured production organization of 190 employees with fifteen supervisors on three shifts to 170 employees with eleven supervisors on two shifts while accommodating 20% increase in sales and workload.
- Streamlined procedures integrating related creative functions under fewer supervisors. Created multi-skilled technicians to avoid overstaffing. Annual profit increased from $65,000 to $750,000 in two years.
- Reversed operating losses in group producing $360,000 in annual sales. Increased group sales to $1,365,000. Workforce reduced from eleven to eight; group is now a profit leader.
- Authored purchasing/receiving/inventory control program to reduce inventory on hand by 50%, to $225,000. Upgraded requisition system from numbered adhesive tags to electronic entry. Revision allowed first accurate P&L reports.

MANAGEMENT, HUMAN RESOURCES

- Instituted revolutionary employee evaluation procedure to include employee in performance analysis, goal setting, and determination of wage adjustment. Ninety-five percent of employees rated themselves more critically (and requested smaller wage increases) than under previous system.
- Eliminated historic animosity between first and second shift personnel through structured team activity and promotion concept of "sixteen-hour work cycle" to replace existing attitudes of two competing shifts.
- Identified critical system failure—order writers not trained in production methods and capabilities. Over 20% of orders impossible to complete as written. Instituted scheduled training program; erroneous orders still declining.

Combined

Resume Example #16 continued

CREATIVE PROBLEM SOLVING
- Conceived, developed, and produced photographically generated color sample booklets to resolve client frustrations when specifying photographic color from process ink samples in standard PMS color swatch books.
- Produced 12-foot-high black and white mural from vertical crop of 16mm movie frame; heavily retouched intermediate 20" x 24" print. Copy negative of retouched print produced mural in three sections through fine mezzotint screen. Mural still on display.
- Provided display text in Arabic, German, and Russian using New York-based translation services and foreign-language typesetters. Obtained necessary entry permits and approvals; produced export documents. Arranged pre-paid services.
- Produced full-color mural to be self-supporting in traveling use as backdrop for mall fashion shows. Mural in sections, plus supporting devices, fit into carrying case less than 36" x 36".

BROKEN DOWN INTO CATEGORIES

PROGRAM DESIGN
- Consulted with over two hundred varied clients in need of A/V programs of all types, sizes, and budgets. Advised appropriate use of overhead transparencies vs. 35mm, computer, or optical slices; guided style and format selection. Produced roughs or storyboards from scripts or notes.
- Restructured production system and quotation to produce environmental graphics for client hospital when original quote of $400,000 proved beyond budget tolerance. Project completed for $160,000.
- Managed graphic production of major space museum project at Jackson Community College. Schedule allowed six weeks from receipt of text, NASA transparencies, and artifacts to opening. Installation completed prior to opening.

EMPLOYMENT HISTORY

1998 - Present	Wonderfully Creative	Director of Production
1992 - 1998	Graphic Designs, Inc.	Manager, Design and Display
1980 - 1984	Somewhat Creative Designs, Ltd.	Graphics Manager
		Director of Show Services
1974 - 1980	Detroit Edison Company	Export Manager
	Graphic Designer	Account Representative

MANAGEMENT DEVELOPMENT PROGRAMS

Statistical Process Control—Oakland University
The Deming Method—George Washington University
Investment in Excellence—Pacific Institute
Effective Team Facilitation—J. Farr
American Economic System—Oakland University
Managing Stress—R. Goren
Communicating for Action—T. Stafford
Statistical Thought Process—Beta Association

COMPENSATES FOR THE LACK OF A COLLEGE DEGREE

EDUCATION   Advertising Design—Center for Creative Studies

Combined

Resume Example #17: Finance
A mid-level manager looking to make a substantial jump in responsibility.

Eric von Hohauser

79 Brampton Street
Bismarck, North Dakota 58010

Res. 701/555-1001
vonman@northern.com

Business Experience:

Over twenty years of administrative and sales management in finance and insurance. Consistent record of improving financial results, operational effectiveness, and customer service.

As *Financial Services Manager* for **LIFE ENHANCE INSURANCE COMPANY**, responsible on a national basis for new account installations, new business development, and marketing of financial products. Conduct seminar presentations to potential customer groups on a variety of financial topics relating to our product capabilities. Extremely knowledgeable concerning all phases of consumer lending regulations. Headed up project and marketed microcomputer system that has since been installed in over 300 credit unions. Designed and implemented an IRA product that has been sold to over 100 credit unions in first six months. 1998–Current

> HIGHLIGHTS SALES AND PROJECT MANAGEMENT CAPABILITIES

While at **LAUREL SCHOOLS CREDIT UNION**, was Operations Officer directly responsible for internal operations of this $22 million financial institution with 33 employees. Was *Chief Operating Officer*; personally administered all lending activities, accounting, staff training, loan delinquencies, and workflow scheduling. Implemented revolving credit loan system. Designed marketing promotions and more efficient services resulting in assets increasing from $10 million to $22 million in two years. 1994–1998

While at **MANUFACTURERS BANK** originated and handled underwriting for short-term commercial construction loans; supervised $22 million portfolio. Designed operating procedures for branch office and main office departments. Developed procedures for implementation of Master Charge system, conducted training sessions with over 300 branch personnel. Conducted analysis resulting in purchase and installation of such equipment as high-speed check photographing machines, branch camera equipment, and teller machines. 1987–1994

> SHOWS ABILITY TO LEARN AND GROW

Began as *Management Trainee* at **HAYDEN & RUIZ** quickly looping through all sales, administration, and operations groups in 18 months, was selected to fill new operations position responsible for identifying and acting on all work flow opportunities. In three and a half years in this position was able to significantly impact speed of customer service, quality of information/data available to staff to make decisions and reduce operating expenses. 1983–1987

> EACH OF THE ABOVE PARAGRAPHS ILLUSTRATES A COMPLEMENTARY SET OF SKILLS THAT HIGHLIGHTS ERIC'S VERSATILITY

Education:

BBA–1983, University of Miami, Business Administration.

Community Activities:

Chairman, Administrative committee for St. Michael's Parish.
Member, Citizens Advisory Group for Board of Education.

Functional

Resume Example #18: Finance
A recent college graduate who makes an excellent representation of her brief but relevant work experience.

Beverly Meadows

147 Deerwood Lane   (309) 555-0001
Cedar Rapids, IA 52404   bevmed@yahoo

Objective | THIS TYPE OF OBJECTIVE IS OK FOR A RECENT GRADUATE |
A position in financial administration, financial analysis, financial planning, or funds management that will require my best efforts.

Education
BA, Financial Administration, June 2003
Iowa State University–GPA: 3.5/4.0

Employment Experience
Summers 2001 & 2003. Holt Corp., Alpha Insulation Division, Iowa City.

| WELL-WRITTEN STATEMENTS DEMONSTRATING A BROAD RANGE OF EXPERIENCE |

- *Financial Analyst:* Analyzed operating, pricing, and purchasing variances weekly. Prepared financial performance reports. Provided financial analysis for special projects. Took part in year-end closing and LIFO cost calculations.
- *Inventory Control:* Planned and conducted verification systems for the Direct Salesforce to report status of inventories accurately. Audited and reconciled inventories of the vans, mini-warehouses, and regional warehouses. Recommended methods to reduce inventory shrinkage.
- *Credit Analyst:* Responsible for USA Direct Sell operations. Approved or rejected sales orders from customers. Reviewed and revised customer credit limits. Wrote 80-page procedure manual for the Credit Department to help establish a consistent credit policy. Negotiated special rates with the collection agencies.

Positions Held While Attending College | CLEVER AND CREATIVE HEADING |

| MAKING THE MOST OF LIMITED EXPERIENCE |

1999–2003 (part-time): Iowa State University Library
Student Assistant: Duties included processing journals, checking out assigned reading and general books, door checking, and shelving books.

2002 (summer): March Companies, Inc., Iowa City
Route Driver: Vacation relief driver; also filled in for terminated salespeople. Responsibilities included selling, delivering, accounting, banking, inventory control, and customer services.

2000 (summer): Karmond Lumber Co., Cedar Rapids
Customer Service: Assisted customers in filling their orders, trained new employees, stocked merchandise, took inventories, and made deliveries to customers' homes.

Honors and Activities

Dean's Honor List, seven terms
Volunteer Income Tax Assistance
Iowa State Finance Club Membership Director

Combined

Resume Example #19: Technical
An impressive array of technical skills and business applications.

Devon H. McCormick

521 E. 14th St., #11H
New York, NY 10009
(212) 529-2418

AN IMPRESSIVE ARRAY OF TECHNICAL SKILLS

Hardware

Workstation: Sun Sparc 10 & 20, Sun 3/110, 3/60, RS/6000; E & S PS300. Mainframe: IBM 3090-600, 4341-II, 360/143, 370/145; DEC PDP-8, PDP-10; Alliant FX/8. PC: IBM PC-XT, PC-AT, '386, '486.

Software

Unix, emacs, Applix, Excel, Sybase, LaTex, JCL, VTAM, VSAM, TSO/ISPF, MVS, MS-DOS 1.0-6.2, X Windows, Motif.

Languages

C, C++, Korn shell, awk, SQL, APL2, APL2/PC, Sharp APL, Sharp APL/PC, STSC APL+PC, STSC APL+II, STSC APL Plus Unix, Sax, Aspect, BAL, BASIC, COBOL, FORTRAN, perl.

Experience

CLEAR, CHRONOLOGICAL FORMAT

Bankers Trust–Assistant Vice President–Senior P/A   November 1996 to present

Design and enhance forecasting models for stocks, bonds, and currencies for eleven countries, in APL and S-Plus:

- mean-variance optimize model allocations with GAMS (General Algebraic Modeling System) optimizer
- analyze economic factors and attribute performance in Excel
- establish and maintain production databases using feeds from various data providers
- analyze risk and perform portfolio recommendations using Barra

Smith Barney–Assistant Vice President–Senior P/A   June 1992 to November 1996

Analyzed, designed, and coded Unix (Sun OS, Solaris, AIX) systems in C, C++, Korn shell, awk, and SQL (Sybase) for Global Risk Management and Mortgage Backed Securities areas, and front-end trading, position and risk management applications for Mortgage Products (e.g., pass-throughs, ARMs, CMOs, derivatives).

- collaborated with traders to specify systems requirements, explained and evangelized system, troubleshot day-to-day problems
- calculated prepayment speeds, reconciled start-of-day positions
- designed Motif screens using UIMX; maintained and modified GUIs in C++
- wrote and maintained rate-of-return calculator, OAS model, prepayment model, core analytical library
- developed and deployed information system to branch offices across the country and in London
- ported mainframe batch tape processing to RS/6000s
- created architect back-office position load with error reporting and recovery
- established coding standards
- designed development environment for testing, quality assurance and production rollover.

BULLETED ACCOMPLISHMENTS ARE EASY TO READ

Combined

Devon H. McCormick

ISS/Futrak (MYCA)–Senior Programmer/Analyst · · · · · · · · · July 1991 to April 1992

- debugged, maintained and developed financial package for risk management
- wrote modules for foreign exchange and for pricing various financial instruments (e.g., bonds, swaps and option-based instruments)
- set up code control and maintenance system
- handled troubleshoot problems with customers in trading rooms and by phone
- analyzed, planned and implemented relational database conversion.

Daedalus Systems–Independent Consultant · · · · · · · · · · August 1989 to July 1991

- converted risk management system for use on Novell network
- debugged, enhanced and verified engineering system for pressure vessel design, in APL2 under VM, to comply with ASME specs (for Mobil Research)
- analyzed CICS to TSO conversion (for GE)
- upgraded Sharp APL system (for Citibank)
- trained PC users.

Morgan Stanley & Co., Inc.–Programmer/Analyst · · · · · · · · July 1987 to August 1989

- used APL and C on Unix system to maintain and develop tools for equities trading system
- developed tools in APL2 for investigating chaos theory
- transferred data and APL programs between various APLs on mainframe and Unix system
- ported real-time equities trading system from mainframe Sharp APL to Unix based APL (Sax)
- created daily automatic tasks to upload data from remote databases.

Citibank, N.A.–Assistant Vice President · · · · · · · · · · August 1981 to July 1987

- installed and maintained Sharp APL and MVS systems
- monitored and optimized system performance
- planned capacity and maintained communications, protocol converters, and other devices for worldwide network of 2 interactive financial reporting systems having over 100 users
- performed troubleshoot APL financial application and system problems
- resolved user access problems for worldwide online systems
- documented maintenance and operations procedures
- collaborated with team to port financial reporting system from STSC to Sharp APL

Education

BA in Philosophy from Vassar College, 1981.
Passed Series 7 and Series 63 securities tests; candidate for CFA.

Related Experience and Skills · · · RELEVANT "EXTRAS"

- Developed curriculum, organized and taught classes on Unix, coding and development standards.
- Studied C++ with the New York PC Users Group C SIG.
- Publicity chair for the APL '89 international conference held in New York.
- Chairman of 4th and 5th annual "APL as a Tool of Thought" professional development seminars (1986 and 1987); provided electronic publicity for seminars 1992–1994.
- Officer of NY/SIGAPL (New York Special Interest Group on APL): chairman 1988/89.
- Panelist at APL '90 on "APL Thinking." Member ACM, NY/ACM, NY/SIGAPL.
- Read and speak French and some Spanish.

Chronological

Resume Example #20: Technical
A high-tech professional with extensive project management experience.

Sigmund A. Rosenthal

9805 Clyde Ct.
Vienna, VA 2218

(914) 907-2904
e-mail: sigr@aol.com

SUMMARY   [CLEAR AND TO THE POINT]

IT management; integration of IT into general business applications; large project management; Web, client/server & distributed processing development; data base systems; standards & processes, and cross-platform (mainframe/mini/PC) systems.

PROFESSIONAL ACCOMPLISHMENTS

2001–Present   Morgan Stanley   [ACTION VERBS DESCRIBE ACCOMPLISHMENTS]   *Consultant*
Established Project Management Office:

- created classification of projects based on size, risk, and related factors;
- defined development and management procedures based on that classification;
- reviewed/managed projects to effect transition to and compliance with new standards;
- designed database for major project with ERWin.

1999–2000   USWeb/CKS Cornerstone   *Senior Project Manager*
Managed team (employees and contractors) to determine business needs, define requirements, specify architecture, design/develop large (~200 screen templates, multi-platform back-end interfaces), web-based, SQL server e-business product for major financial client.
Responsible for:

- determining and documenting business requirements,
- creation of information and infrastructure architecture,
- defining programming and documentation standards,   [RESPONSIBILITIES]
- screen treatment, design and navigation,
- design and programming of web site,
- employee training and development,
- selection, sizing of hardware, software, and communications network.

1999   Morgan Stanley   *Consultant*
Assessed IT organization structure and recommended changes (organization, practices and tools) to aid transition from legacy, mainframe based development to RAD (Rapid Application Development), Client/Server, and Web-based development. Coordinated SEI CMM study.

1997–1999   New York City Transit Authority   *Special Consultant to CIO (VP)*
Redesigned technology infrastructure and software architecture. Created small Client/Server application to demonstrate new paradigm. Introduced Visual Basic, HTML, ActiveX. Supported Data WareHouse, and Digital Imaging exploratory committees.

1991–1997   Cubic Corporation–MetroCard   *Software Director (80+ Staff)*
Senior IS executive (reporting directly to President) with P&L responsibility for development and operation of fare collection system for New York subways & buses. This was a large, complex, 24x7 system incorporating the latest technology including magnetic tickets & smart cards, consisting of IBM mainframes (MVS, CICS, DB2 & COBOL) hosting an LU6.2 WAN of PCs and AIX systems, each acting as a server with its own LAN of client devices in a client/server environment. System was developed by multiple teams on both coasts. Project was delivered on time and within budget.

Combined

Sigmund A. Rosenthal   Page 2 of 3

Responsible for:
- identifying business needs and convincing client of their value
- defining requirements to satisfy agreed to business objectives
- contract negotiations with client to deliver product that satisfied needs `MORE RESPONSIBILITIES`
- contract negotiations with multiple subcontractors to develop portions of product
- design, programming, testing, installation, and operation of automated system
- outsourcing subsystem development
- coordinating efforts of multiple suppliers
- re-engineering of accounting
- acquisition and sizing of hardware and communications
- managing project totaling over $13 million billing; exceeded profit target

Selected by chairman as part of special management team to create a new subsidiary corporation.

1982–1991   Computer Software Innovations Group, Ltd.   *President*

Identified market needs and defined products for client companies.

1990–91: Developed testing course for organizations using object oriented techniques. Invited to speak at Object Expo '92

1990–91: IBM sub-contractor: reviewed management of 200+ staff project to streamline management structure and procedures.

1986–91: Sub-contractor to P&YI (under contract to MCI): developed and taught courses in technical management, project planning, testing and Quality Assurance. Established Q.A. organization. Defined methodologies and standards.

1986–88: Bell Communications Research: designed and developed business model and relational architecture for corporate database to be implemented in DB2. Selected CASE tool for requirements project. Taught use of UNIX.

1982–86: Bell Laboratories: researched and implemented effective transfer of software inspections and other software engineering and QA techniques to over 40 development projects involving over 1,000 staff members. Developed and taught inspections and testing courses. Measured results: 30% reduction in development time, 80% in error rates.

1974–1982   IBM Corporation

1980–82: Instructor, Systems Science Institute
- designed and taught management and software engineering courses to senior data processing management and staff
- performed research in software engineering, identified best practices

1978–80: Systems Engineering Manager, N.Y. Banking Office
- managed two teams of Systems Engineers: one of financial experts, the other technical specialists
- planned branch office staffing and training
- recognized as one of top 10% of IBM's S.E. Managers

1976–78: Teleprocessing Specialist, New York Region
- reviewed/approved communication proposals and network design for technical accuracy
- conducted courses in Communications Management, SNA

Combined

(914) 907-2904
e-mail: sigr@aol.com

1974–76: Project Manager, Financial Office
- designed and managed implementation (in major New York City financial institution) of first SNA network shipped by IBM
- The project was delivered on time, and the network and methods developed by me were adopted by IBM as models for similar projects

EDUCATION AND HONORS

> STRONG ACADEMIC INTERESTS AND CREDENTIALS

Cornell University   IBM Systems Research Institute
University of Connecticut   Member, Sigma Xi, National Science Honorary Society.
MA, Mathematics   Member, M.A.A., Mathematical Association of America.
IBM Management School
BS, Mathematics Cum Laude

PUBLICATIONS

"What's the Object?", *Object Oriented Hotline*, December, 1991.
"Improving the Performance of Software Development Organizations," *ComputerWorld*, 2/19/1990.

REFERRAL QUOTE

"Sig possesses a rare combination of technical and managerial experience nurtured by a keen intelligence and disarming personal skills. He is a results-oriented software development manager, accustomed to completing projects on time and within budget. He is also an inspirational leader who knows how to select, direct, and train his staff."

—Arthur D. Rosenberg, ADR Documentation, Inc.

ADDITIONAL KEYWORDS: Java Script, VB, Intranet, Internet, Web, Network, Data Warehouse, DHTML, XML, CSS, GUI, MS Office, MS Project, VBA, Word, Excel, VSS, Data modeling

> KEYWORDS ARE INTENDED TO GET A "HIT" FROM ELECTRONIC SEARCHES CONDUCTED BY EMPLOYMENT AND CONSULTING AGENTS

Resume Example #21: Technical
Hardware and software skills focusing on pharmaceutical applications.

Wojciech Szewczyk

21 Parkway Place
Parlin, NJ 08859

email@home.com

Phone: Home (732) 727-6739
Office (908) 298-4556

SUMMARY:
SIGNIFICANT RESPONSIBILITIES

Data processing professional with over 20 years of experience as a system analyst, software developer and project leader in Windows PC and mainframe environment.

Excellent design, analytical and programming skills. Heavy concentration in client-server systems and relational database design. Hands-on experience in all aspects of information systems life cycle, from business requirement definition to final implementation and maintenance.

Specializing in web and VB applications and intersystem connections in client-server environment: ASP, ADO, JavaScript, Vbscript, VB, ORACLE, ODBC, Front Page, MS Access.

HARDWARE: PC, IBM Mainframes, HP9000, VAX, PDP11

SOFTWARE: Active Server Pages, VB script, Java script, Visual Basic, MS Access, Front Page, Oracle SQL, SQL-Plus, PL/SQL, ODBC, Crystal Reports, Windows 2000, Windows NT, DB2, SAS, REXX, Fortran, Cobol, JCL, MVS, Inquire, VAX Assembler, TCP/IP-FTP.

PROFESSIONAL EXPERIENCE:

1988–current   ***Schering Plough Corporation,* Kenilworth, NJ**

• *Web enabled LIMS reports.*
Developed internet application using ASP and ADO for 30+ reports for ORACLE-based LIMS system containing Stability data (used to forecast drug expiration dates). Used Crystal Reports, Stored procedures. Client-server environment consisted of ASP, ADO, Windows NT, ORACLE and Crystal Reports.

• *Internet application for tracking recertification documents.*
Designed and implemented web application to retrieve certificates of analysis issued to extend expiration dates for specific products. Search based on product Id. System developed in Visual Interdev using ASP, Java script and VB script; retrieved data stored in MS Access database.

• *Visual Basic front end to Crystal Reports.*
Designed and developed VB application enabling selection of report and enter parameters. Parameters passed to SQL server stored procedures, which populated ADO recordsets in VB. Crystal reports based on database independent ADO recordsets. Application uses Visual Basic, ADO recordsets, SQL server stored procedures, Crystal Reports.

• *Inventory Bar Code system.*
As project leader/project manager, gathered and analyzed requirements, design hardware and ORACLE database architecture. Proposed budget, purchased equipment, performed LAN generation, programming, testing, and implementation of Inventory Bar Code system. System uses Visual Basic to gather information from bar code readers identifying dispensed substance, and from scales used to weigh required amount of ingredients to manufacture Clinical Trial batches. Transaction data stored in ORACLE database. Project part of Y2K effort.

DESCRIPTIVE EXPLANATIONS OF
ACCOMPLISHMENTS PRESENTED
IN A MEANINGFUL CONTEXT

Chronological

- *Equipment cleaning validation system.*
Designed and implemented client-server system for tracking Clinical Batch equipment cleaning process. Project scope included hardware architecture design, software and hardware evaluation and recommendation, budgeting and purchasing, network configuration and database architecture design. Database designed as collection of the DB2 and Access tables accessed throughout ODBC connectivity. Environment consisted of DB2/ODBC, MVS, NETWARE LAN, MS Access. Software written in Visual Basic.

- *Interface to Stability LIMS system.*
Gathered requirements, designed and implemented system transferring data from Excel spreadsheets populated by HP chromatography systems to MS Access database for review by group leaders. Approved data extracted from Access database and uploaded to Unix server. Software written in Visual Basic using Access and Oracle databases.

- *Clinical Batches Manufacturing tracking system.*
Designed, coded, implemented, documented and maintained Batch Record Tracking system. System keeps track of batch life cycle information. Technical environment consists of DB2, SAS, Inquire, REXX, MVS, JCL, ISPF.

- *Clinical Environment Monitoring System.*
Designed and implemented system collecting environment data including temperature, humidity, pressure, and particle count in rooms used for clinical batches manufacture and storage. System displays, prints alarm information when parameters are out of limits. Collected data used to generate trend charts in Excel. Technical environment consisted of VAX Assembler, pathworks, PC, Excel.

1985–1987   *Medco Containment (Merck's subsidiary),* **Fair Lawn, NJ**
Developed and coded mail order system for prescription drugs in COBOL on Unisys.

1976–1985   *Warsaw Technical University,* **Warsaw Poland**
Performed mathematical modeling in FORTRAN and Assembler using PDP1140.

EDUCATION:

Ph.D. in Computer Science, 1984–Warsaw Technical University, Poland
M.S. in Computer Science, 1974–Warsaw Technical University, Poland

TOP-LEVEL ACADEMIC CREDENTIALS

Resume Example #22: Executive
An executive who gets it all onto a single page.

Roger M. Northman

14 McCaul Street
Toronto, Ontario MST 1WI

Home (416) 555-1514
RMNorth@aei.ca

Professional Experience

1993-Present

PUBLISHERS ASSOCIATED SERVICES, INC., Toronto, Ontario
President and Principal - Promote and furnish cost-efficient microcomputer systems to publishing companies. Assist in selection of appropriate hardware and software designed to save time and control costs. Increase editorial and marketing productivity.

> HE SAYS A LOT WITH A FEW WELL-CHOSEN WORDS

1989-1993

THOMAS PUBLICATIONS, Toronto, Ontario

> WHEN YOU HAVE ACCOMPLISHED THIS MUCH, DETAILS CAN BE SAFELY SUMMARIZED

President and CEO - Chief executive in charge of operations for a leading vocational/technical textbook publisher. Exercised P&L authority for all phases of management, including editorial, production, and marketing, with seventy employees reporting.

Executive Vice-President: Reporting to the Chairman of the Board Administered daily operations of Mardel Publishers in Albany, NY. Position combined general management authority with supervision of marketing and sales staff. Established computerized sales information systems, resulting in better allocation of sales territories and improvements in capital investment in publishing projects.

Director, Marketing and Sales: Directed all marketing activities, including advertising, direct mail promotion, product releases, exhibits, and field selling. Developed computer database of mailing list, and organized sales communication system for timely reportage by field sales representatives.

1984-1989

O'BRIEN-HULL BOOK COMPANY OF CANADA, Toronto, Ontario
Held key positions in marketing and sales administration with three textbook divisions: Goutt, Collegiate Community, and Vocational/ Technical. Achievements include development of first integrated product information system for college and technical/vocational ties. Introduced Professional Selling Skills program to college travelers; designed and published *Technical Education News* quarterly magazine; instrumental in converting catalogs to computer database for electronic typesetting.

Education

1986—M.B.A., University of Toronto Graduate School of Business
   Administration
1984—B.A., McGill University, Montreal

Chronological

11 Cordial Avenue
Ridgefield Park, New Jersey 07660

knowsit@att.com
Home (201) 555-9876
Office (201) 555-0001

NOAH A. LOTTS

Objective:	Senior Corporate Planner, General Manager, or Chief Marketing Officer

**DIVISIONAL
VICE PRESIDENT**

PULLING ALL THE ELEMENTS
TOGETHER: IMPACT, SKILLS,
ACCOUNTABILITY,
EXPERIENCE, SUCCESS

Profit and loss responsibility for corporation with annual sales volume of $76 million. Corporation acquired by growing conglomerate resulting in restructured sales organization, leading to expanded market reach. Developed new market strategy, added new sales representatives, dropped two unprofitable products and added three new products. Strategy allowed for 21% sales increase and profit increase of $3.7 million.

**MARKETING,
PRODUCTION, AND
GENERAL
MANAGEMENT**

- *Initiated* and *managed* design and implementation of new product line with eventual sales record of $12.7 million over first two years.
- *Developed* and *implemented* three-year plan to upgrade efficiency of extensive line operation including a capital expenditure commitment of $9.3 million. INNOVATIVE
- *Decreased* $900,000 accounts receivable collections from 87-day average to less than 35 days.
- *Initiated* improving scheduling system resulting in reduction of delivery time by half.

**VICE PRESIDENT
CORPORATE
PLANNING**

IT WOULD BE DIFFICULT
TO FORMULATE MORE
IMPRESSIVE
ACCOMPLISHMENTS
THAN THESE

- *Introduced* "Results Oriented Management" (MBO) approach to $750 million insurance company that led to a bottom line increase of 29% during a down economy.
- *Developed* and *implemented* $310 million acquisition program over five-year period utilizing stock/tax advantages leading to R.O.I. improvement of 19%.
- *Created* product development group, which delivered six new insurance programs over three-year period leading to sales of $19 million and profit of $31 million.

**CHIEF
MARKETING
OFFICER**

PROBLEM SOLVING

- *Conceived* of and *marketed* credit card program leading to $131 million in gross revenues over four-year period.
- *Developed* award-winning advertising program with annual budget of $9 million.
- *Revamped* product line that had suffered loss of 15% in market share, resulting in recapture of 27% of market over three-and-a-half-year period.
- *Reorganized* forty-seven-member sales organization, allowing for increased field time and reduced travel, and resulting in a decrease in sales expenditures of $1.5 million in one year.

Combined

NOAH A. LOTTS
Page 2

EMPLOYMENT HISTORY	1994 - PRESENT	Executive Vice President Sales & Marketing	Cubic Systems Bloomfield, New Jersey
	1988 - 1994	Vice President Corporate Planning	Quadrangle International, Hoboken, New Jersey
	1979 - 1988	Sales Manager	Gotham Insurance, Inc. Wilmington, Delaware
	1971 - 1979	Loan Officer	Metal Specialties Corp., Syracuse, New York
	1968 - 1971	Bank Teller	First National Bank, Hartford, Connecticut
MILITARY SERVICE	1966 - 1968	1st Lieutenant, Communications	U.S. Army
EDUCATION	1965	Bachelor of Arts Business Administration	New York University
FOREIGN LANGUAGES	Spanish, Portuguese, French		

TELLING WHAT YOU'VE DONE
WITH DIGNITY . . . WHEN THERE
IS A GOOD DEAL TO TALK ABOUT

Combined

Resume Example #24: Senior Executive
A senior-level executive who effectively highlights her successes in the international arena.

Constance Worldy

1696 SOUTH FOURTH STREET
PHILADELPHIA, PENNSYLVANIA 19147

RESIDENCE: (215)321-2121
MYWORLD@WORLDNET.COM

MODESTLY STATED

Objective

Resourceful, results-oriented executive accustomed to profit and loss responsibilities seeks domestic or international marketing position, preferably in high-tech materials manufacturing.

Background Summary

COMPREHENSIVE SUMMARY

Extensive experience principally at executive level in international and domestic marketing, manufacturing, and engineering research and development, for $115 million manufacturer of precision specialty metal products. Strengths in development of production facilities and licensees in Europe and the Far East. Distinguished record in new product development and patents. Solid background in managing start-up and ongoing production operations.

ACTION PHRASES SUPPORT
OBJECTIVE AND SUMMARY

Career History

MONOLITHIC INDUSTRIES, Philadelphia, Pennsylvania   1987 - PRESENT
Vice President, International Operations: 1998 - PRESENT
Direct overseas marketing and licensees in Europe and Asia for manufacturer of bearings and friction materials. Annual revenue from licensees up to $25 million.

- Instructed Japanese licensee on bearing manufacturing processes including powder-making, strip sintering, and related operations. Increased license fees by 315% per year.
- Designed and arranged financing for $16 million bearings manufacturing plant in India, generating a $5.5 million profit on $14 million in equipment sales.
- Researched market, established process, and designed manufacturing facility for low-cost production of cam bushings in mainland China for $37 million worldwide market.

GENERAL MANAGER, BEARINGS DIVISION: 1995 - 1998

MEASURABLE RESULTS

Profit and loss responsibility for all operations, including manufacturing, quality, engineering, finance, personnel, and marketing. Annual sales $60 million. Staff of eight hundred in four facilities.

- Restructured division on a product-line basis generating an additional 8% gross margin, reducing inventory $3 million, and increasing profits by $2.5 million from a loss position in first year of operation.
- Directed start-up of production at 100,000 square foot manufacturing plant.
- Increased market share to 60% at three major automobile companies in a declining market.

Chronological

Constance Worldy **Page 2**

DIRECTOR OF SALES AND MARKETING: 1992 - 1995
Directed marketing program for OEM bearings and transmission parts. Annual sales: $75 million.
- Organized and staffed complete marketing activity. Sales growth compounded at 17% per year ($10 to $40 million) in nine years; non-automotive sales increased 300%.
- Established European licensees resulting in a $9.5 million equipment order in Rumania, licensees in France and Germany, plus new major customer accounts.

> PROGRESSION OF RESPONSIBILITIES

DIRECTOR OF RESEARCH AND DEVELOPMENT: 1987 - 1990
Directed materials research, process development, and customer engineering activities.
- Developed unique asbestos-free, paper-based friction materials generating $15 million sales (60% gross profit).
- Analyzed process for sintering of copper-lead on steel strip yielding a 300% increase in output and 40% cost reduction for a $11 million annual savings.

ALLOYS, INCORPORATED; Jennings, Iowa [SHOWS SOLID TECHNICAL BACKGROUND] 1981 - 1987
RESEARCH METALLURGIST
Studied wear and fatigue properties of metals. Developed new materials involving the sintering and casting of non-ferrous metals.

EDUCATION
University of Nebraska - B.S., Physics and Mathematics
Advanced Management Training courses on Manufacturing Strategy at Harvard University Business School and at Iowa State University Graduate School of Sales and Marketing.

PATENTS AND PUBLICATIONS

> A PROSPECTIVE EMPLOYER WILL WANT TO KNOW THE DETAILS IN AN INTERVIEW

Twenty-one patents dealing with materials and processes.
Numerous articles in a variety of technical and marketing publications.

ASSOCIATIONS
Society of Automotive Engineers - American Society for Metals.

Chronological

Resume Example #25: Senior Executive
A retired executive seeking part-time consulting work.

Isaac E. Elder

25 Cedar Lane   Home: (919) 555-0001
Raleigh, NC 27602   olddude@neolith.com

Objective

To apply my extensive management, problem-solving, marketing and interpersonal skills in a consulting capacity to selected sales and marketing organizations.

> SPECIFIC AND DESCRIPTIVE

Summary of Accomplishments

> ACCOMPLISHMENTS SUPPORT OBJECTIVE

- Doubled sales in capacity as marketing director during a three-year down economy (1995–2001).

  > CONSISTENCY

- Redesigned and regrouped over one hundred sales/marketing brochures into 20 coordinated pamphlets that won *Marketing Age* magazine's "Award of Excellence."
- Managed one of nine national sales regions consistently number one for 21 quarters (1979–1983).
- Active member of National Machine Tool Builders Association. Headed technical update sub-committee (1991–1997).

  > PEOPLE SKILLS

- Named St. Louis Business Alliance "Public Speaker of the Year" (1993 & 1996).
- Started St. Louis Business Alliance mentoring program linking over 300 volunteer executives with high school and college students.
- Recognized as developer of effective sales representatives. "Salesman of the Year" came from my region 3 out of 4 years.

  > RESPONSIBILITY

- Prepared, managed, and monitored corporate marketing budget exceeding $3.2 million.
- Developed and assisted in leading over 200 sales representatives through a 3-week "Sales Excellence" training program.

Employment History

CROSBY MACHINE TOOL CORPORATION; Abilene, Texas
Marketing Vice President (1995-2001)

MCDOUGLAS AND CARTY CORPORATION; St. Louis, Missouri
Sales Manager (1972–1995)

U.S. ARMY—Lieutenant (1968–1972)

Education

B.S.—Business Administration; University of Kansas; Topeka, Kansas (1967)

> A LONG AND SUCCESSFUL CAREER SUMMARIZED IN A SINGLE PAGE

Combined

Emory X. Perience

343 High Road
New Route, Pennsylvania 19400

exp@maturity.com
(610) 555-9673

Executive with over 25 years experience in service companies, including turnarounds, mergers and acquisitions, systems development, marketing, and sales, who reversed a company loss of $7 million into a $2.1 million profit on a sales increase of $22 million.

RESPONSIBILITY AND
ACCOUNTABILITY

CAREER SUMMARY

Proven leadership in sales, marketing, customer service, and public relations; speaker/guest lecturer. Team motivator with ability to recruit, build, and retain staff. Managed staffs from forty-five to five hundred associates. Past and present member of Board of Directors of eight organizations of which three are system development/integration companies. Bachelor of Science degree in Management from Michigan State University. Graduate study at University of Texas at Arlington.

PROFESSIONAL HIGHLIGHTS

- Directed private investment/corporate development group through three acquisitions and four refinancings; sales exceeded $300M.
- Created alliance of four data communications corporations to form $90 million sales organization.
- Acquired two computer service companies
- Secured major long-term facilities management contracts.
- Significant contributor in reduction of operating losses of $6.2M to $1.5M to breakeven in two years.

Hands-on operations, product management, systems management experience resulting in increased profitability.
- Developed client/server and mainframe software products for national marketplace in credit card, collections, loan origination, loan tracking, float management service, and national check processing company utilizing image capture technology.
- Directed successful portation of software package to new platform generating new sales. Sixty person-year effort.
- Re-engineered major West Coast bank's cash management services. Benefits exceeded $10M annually.
- Organized functional departments into business units.
- Developed multiple strategic product plans including technology and new markets.
- Managed computer services company with five locations.
- Project management of multiple engagements that exceeded 100 person-years.
- Purchased and administered over $220 million in capital equipment and software contracts.
- Managed and controlled over 1,200 application conversions including four international installations.
- Planned, designed, and constructed a state-of-the-art computer center and headquarters facility.

A SOMEWHAT
DIFFERENT FORMAT

Combined

A GRADUAL AND BELIEVABLE
PROGRESSION OF SKILLS AND
RESPONSIBILITIES

PROFESSIONAL EXPERIENCE

COOPER, HYATT AND CO; Radnor, Pennsylvania (2000–Present)　　　　**Product Director**
Consulting and systems development company. Subsidiary of Premier Financial Systems.

LIBERTY SOLUTIONS, Bryn Mawr, Pennsylvania (1998–2000)　　　　**Managing Director**
Systems integration and software development company. Subsidiary of Quadrant Scientifics (NYSE).

HAMPTON ENTERPRISES, Ann Arbor, Michigan (1995–1998)
Hampton Information Systems (1996–1998)　　　　**President and Chief Operating Officer**
Hampton Engineering, Inc. (1995–1996)　　　　**President**
Private investment/corporate development company owned by Charles A. Hampton, Founder of Hampton Publishing and Hampton Financial. Interests in network integration, distribution, technology park development.

GLOBAL DATA CORPORATION, Auburn Hills, Michigan (1985–1995)
(1986–1995)　　　　**Vice President, General Manager and Director**
(1975)　　　　**Director of Systems and Programming**
Financial services facilities management, automated services and software development firm. Subsidiary of Global Bancorp Inc.

CINCOM SYSTEMS, Cincinnati, Ohio (1983–1985)
(1985)　　　　**Sales Representative; Dallas, Texas**
(1983–1985)　　　　**Systems Engineer; Dallas, Texas**
A world wide supplier of database and data communications software.

NATIONAL SHAREDATA CORPORATION, Dallas, Texas (1982–1983)　　　　**Systems Engineer**

UNIVERSITY COMPUTING COMPANY, Dallas, Texas (1980–1982)
(1981–1982)　　　　**Project Leader**
(1980)　　　　**Programmer Analyst**
Major software supplier to financial service industry

Yu Sing Yee
100 Bridge Bay Roadway
Brooklyn, NY 11000

email:Sqtsing@law.gov
phone: 718/900–1234
cell: 917/700-4321

SUMMARY

Recently retired member of the New York City Police Department. Achieved rank of Sergeant over an exemplary career of over twenty years. Extensive experience in law enforcement and community relations.

PROFESSIONAL ACCOMPLISHMENTS

September, 1980–May, 2002   New York City Police Department
  Served with distinction over a period of twenty-two years.

> CONSISTENT UPWARD MOVEMENT THROUGH THE RANKS

May, 1997–May, 2002   Sergeant, *Supervisor, Anti-Crime Unit*
  Patrolled assigned neighborhoods in plain clothes to assure public safety. Identified and monitored targeted illegal activities.
  • Supervised four Police Officers.
  • Evaluated performance of team members.

> TRANSFERABLE MANAGEMENT AND SUPERVISORY SKILLS

  • Maintained administrative reports.
  • Conducted investigations.
  • Collaborated with interstate agencies and Police Departments.

July, 1995–May, 1997   Sergeant, *Patrol Supervisor*
  Promoted to Sergeant: worked alternatively as Patrol Supervisor and Desk Officer.
  • Coordinated daily activities of Precinct.
  • Trained new Police Department recruits.
  • Supervised up to thirty Police Officers.
  • Evaluated performance of squad members.
  • Verified arrests, provided emergency services, decided varied courses of action.

September, 1985–July, 1995   Detective, *Brooklyn Night Watch*
  Conducted preliminary investigations on all serious incidents, including homicides, serious assaults, bias incidents, and other major crimes. Responsible for analyzing crime scenes, interviewing complainants and witnesses, filing reports and providing notifications to specialized units.

February, 1985–September, 1985   Detective, *Precinct Detective Unit*
  Promoted to Detective rank in December, 1984.

September, 1980–December, 1984   Police Officer

EDUCATION

BS, John Jay College of Criminal Justice (plus extended credits in Accounting).

> STRONG ACADEMIC BACKGROUND

Supplemental training in criminal investigation, homicide investigation, sex crime investigation, dignitary protection.

FOREIGN LANGUAGES   Cantonese

Chronological

Resume Example #28: Chef
An imaginative and creative "blue-collar professional" looking for a better job.

PIERRE CUISINE
MASTER CHEF

14 Boulevard Fourchette
New Orleans, Louisiana

Telephone (mornings)
(504) 555-0544

The proper blend of training and diversified experience is my recipe for culinary excellence!

From the everyday to the extraordinary. After your clientele have tasted my international entrees they will demand an "encore."

> CREATIVE OBJECTIVE FOR A CREATIVE BUSINESS

EXPERIENCE

1997 - Present

Arnaud's Restaurant   **Head Chef**
New Orleans, Louisiana
Manage entire kitchen staff of twenty-two that produces the finest luncheons and dinners in the South.

> EVIDENCE OF MANAGEMENT ABILITIES AND EXPERIENCE

- Create extraordinary seafood, meat, and chicken dishes, specializing in delicate sauces.
- Supervise three assistant chefs and wine steward.
- Oversee training of four apprentices.
- Responsible for purchases of all foods and kitchen budget of $1.4 million.

1993 - 1997

Le Chateau   **Chef**
Charlesbourg, Quebec
One of two chefs directly under head chef
- Prepared special sauces and such delicate specialties as pheasant under glass.
- Served flambées and other spectacular dishes in dining room.
- Conceived and wrote all lunch menus.

1989 - 1993

Chez Paul Beaucoup   **Apprentice Chef**
Paris, France
- Prepared hors d'oeuvres, entrees, and desserts under the direction of one of the world's foremost chefs.
- Assisted in the purchase of foods and kitchen supplies.

EDUCATION

1989

> THE TYPE OF TRAINING THAT STANDS OUT

Diploma, École d'Haute Cuisine, Lyons, France
Generally recognized as the leading cooking school in Europe.

SPECIAL TALENTS

- Capable of serving as a wine steward.
- Fluent French and English; spoken Italian and Spanish.
- Aware of kosher dietary laws.

PERSONAL

> MAKES AN IMPORTANT POINT THAT MIGHT OTHERWISE BE OVERLOOKED

> CLEVER, WITTY, APPEALING

- Dual nationality: French and Canadian.
- Willing to relocate to any civilized country.

Chronological

Resume Example #29: Career Change
An ex-offender who has changed his ways makes even the worst of his experiences work for him.

Rex Conn
12591 Euclid Avenue
East Cleveland, Ohio 44112

barout@freedom.com
Business: (216) 555-1261

> A DELICATE ISSUE IS
> WORDED NICELY

Career Objective:	*To apply my extensive firsthand experience in career and crisis counseling of ex-offenders and probationers which helped them strengthen their lives and make positive adjustments to society.*
Experience:	**COUNSELING:** Considerable experience as a result of over 300 one-on-one counseling sessions with ex-offenders in the areas of career assessment and drug and alcohol abuse.
	PROGRAM DESIGN: Initiated, designed, and implemented a career/life planning workshop that resulted in nearly 220 probationary attendees participating, with over 50% landing jobs within six months of the program's completion.
	LEADERSHIP: Headed up the Prison Reform Board, a sixteen-member state organization designed to improve prison conditions and treatment of inmates.

> SIX ACTION
> STATEMENTS

HUMAN RELATIONS: Developed reputation in working with diverse ethnic/neighborhood groups to encourage probationary individuals to avail themselves of counseling. Written up in *Cleveland Plain Dealer* as a neighborhood activist.

MANAGEMENT: Lead counselor over nine other counselors in evening crisis intervention center. During fourteen months as lead counselor, center handled over 4,000 phone calls and 1,900 walk-ins.

CITIZENSHIP: Secretary for Cleveland Concerned Citizens, a civic organization dedicated to helping ex-offenders establish productive lives in the community.

> PROFESSIONAL CREDENTIALS

MEMBER OF NATIONAL ASSOCIATION OF CAREER COUNSELORS

Education:	Bachelor of Science Degree, to be obtained June 1998, Cleveland State University
	Major in Guidance and Counseling

> IMPORTANT TO INCLUDE

ADDITIONAL EDUCATION: Crisis intervention workshop, through Ohio Guidance and Counseling Association, 1990; seminar entitled "Alcohol and Substance Abuse," sponsored by Cleveland Chapter of National Association of Career Counselors, 1992.

> TRANSFORMS AN
> UNFORTUNATE EXPERIENCE
> INTO A POSITIVE AND
> OPTIMISTIC CAREER

References:	Outstanding references available on request.

> VITAL UNDER THESE CIRCUMSTANCES

Functional

Consulting Resumes

Consulting resumes are different from the other types. Independent contractor, vendor, free agent, consultant—whatever they call nonemployees in your neck of the woods, if you do contract work, you need a resume that elevates your skills and experience to the attention of decision-makers.

What to Include

Most headhunters, consulting agencies, and clients want to see in detail:

- The kind of work you have done (applications, purpose/use)
- The tools (especially technical) and techniques you used to do it
- *If possible*, quantifiable results (completed project on/ahead of deadline and within budget) and value-added accomplishments (improvements, innovations, etc.)
- Level of responsibility, e.g., team/project leader, sole responsibility for . . ., etc.
- Adaptability and problem-solving skills
- Names of clients/industries (provide specific references outside your resume)

Length

Elsewhere in this book we strongly recommend that traditional (i.e., full-time position) resumes be limited to one or two pages. This does not, however, apply to consulting resumes, which must reflect the different kinds of assignments you have successfully completed, with emphasis on those that may be relevant to your current search.

The length and specificity of your consulting resume depends upon the nature and range of your accomplishments and the kind of work you are seeking. If your background and interests are uniquely focused on a few technical specialties, e.g., Java/HTML programming or an exotic area of chemical engineering, you may not need to broaden the scope of your resume. Otherwise, you are advised to adapt it accordingly.

Value Added

Senior consultants are also expected to show an understanding of the priorities and business applications they helped to develop or improve. Value added, such as improvements to the project plan and suggestions made by you that were implemented by the client, increase your perceived value above that of people who blindly follow instructions.

Problem-Solving

Examples of problem-solving skills are definitely the right consulting stuff: state the problem and how you resolved it clearly and succinctly; it will not impress if it cannot be understood by nontechnical readers.

The following three resume samples use the format many leading consulting agencies prefer.

Resume Example #30: Consulting
Additional pages for experienced consultants are appropriate.

Kenneth Francis Walsh

399 Van Wagner Road, Poughkeepsie, NY 12603
Home: 845.452.4081, Cell: 914.299.8007, Fax: 914.471.2675
kfwconsultant@yahoo.com

SUMMARY:

A DETAILED SUMMARY
INTRODUCES AN
EXTENSIVE RESUME

Senior Information Technology Professional with over 19 years of managerial and hands-on experience. Strong project and account management skills enhanced by a thorough familiarity with IT management, disaster recovery and data security. Capable of making Director Level decisions based upon needs of the business.

Software: Project Management Tools (ABT Workbench, MS Project), MS Word, MS Excel, MS PowerPoint, Visio, Documentum, Workstation Tools and Applications, MS FrontPage, Networking, Operating Systems (VM, MVS), Databases (DB2, SQL), Security Software, Security Audits, Capacity/Hardware/Software Planning, Script/REXX.

Functions: Senior Management, Project Planning, Problem Analysis, Problem Determination, Process Evaluations, Customer Relations, Disaster Recovery, Negotiations, Price Waterhouse-Cooper Summit-D Project Management Methodology.

Training: IBM, Project Workbench, Microsoft Project, freelance, Lotus Smart Suite, MS Office, VM, MVS, JCL, PLAS, Assembler, REXX, SNA, VTAM, PVM, RSCS, NETVIEW, RACF, DB2, SQL, MACRO, DIRMAINT, TOOLS, Information Management, Capacity Planning, Hardware Configurations, PriceWaterhouse Cooper Summit-D Project Management Methodology.

PROFESSIONAL EXPERIENCE:

For **RCM Technologies**

3/02–Present: Schering-Plough Corporation   **IT Business Analyst**
Scoped effort to upgrade OS/390 and all down level program products on the Research Institute Services (RIS) mainframe.

- Researched and established method for minimizing impact of applications using SAS.
- Evaluated current regression test scripts toward automation for static environments.
- Determined plan for the future regarding system and program product updates, testing practices and retirement of SAS applications.

THIS IS THE STANDARD FORMAT REQUESTED
BY MANY CONSULTING AGENCIES

Chronological

Kenneth Francis Walsh

For **Pyramid Consulting**

2/01–8/01: F. Hoffmann-La Roche, Limited **Senior Project Manager**
Led effort for development and rollout of Image Workflow System for (PDBI) Pharma-Development Biometric Informatics. The system provided an effective transport and repository mechanism of clinical trial documents with easy, fast access tracking facilities and export facilities to electronic submission for New Drug Approval (NDA), while also supporting the Roche clinical study process.

- Developed status and master project plan using Price Waterhouse-Cooper Summit-D Methodology to roll out Roche's new validated Imaging Workflow System.
- Managed a worldwide team of 24 members located in the US, Switzerland and England.
- Identified testing requirements, tasks on critical path.
- Managed resolution of project issues.
- Communicated project activity with status reports and weekly team meetings.
- Coordinated activities and schedules with third party vendor developing system software.
- Collaborated with Business Team to create User Acceptance Test Package to verify compliance with System Requirements Document and Development Vendor Contract.

ACTION VERBS CLEARLY COMMUNICATE ACTIVITIES AND ACCOMPLISHMENTS

6/00–1/01: InSITE Services, LLC **Director, Information Technology**
Managed two departments for Nation Wide Energy Data Billing and Analysis Company. Applications used by web developers included Cold Fusion, Java, Oracle and Formula One. Team assignments derived by internal business needs as well as cost recovered Client requests.

- . . . one department responsible for maintaining and enhancing proprietary bill processing engine and associated Oracle Database using PowerBuilder, Java and Crystal Reports.
- . . . second department responsible for developing and supporting web Internet access to client data and company intranet HR support structure and tools to facilitate internal support of the Clients.
- Re-engineered processes throughout company: created unique project management methodology to facilitate work throughout entire IT and QA Testing organizations with a team that built and supported a client call center structure and operation.

2/00–5/00: CyberStaff America, Limited **Senior Manager**
Sr. Project Manager for Quality Assurance Department of tri-state consulting firm.

- Built methodology for QA assessments, presentation material, analysis on current consulting engagements.
- Participated in sales meeting as QA expert to provide technical information.
- Managed consultants and interfaced with clients with regard to active accounts.
- Developed web-testing methodology to be used as a new area of business.

For **CyberStaff America, Limited**

11/99–2/00: Ziff-Davis **Senior Project Management**
Managed Y2K Century Global Rollover Plan, including all aspects of IT and Facilities to ensure Business Continuity throughout critical Y2K period. Related and non-related IT Activities were integrated in the plan. Global scope covered 10 locations and 300 servers. *No problems identified post–Y2K.*

Chronological

The Resume Handbook

Kenneth Francis Walsh

4/98–11/99: Walsh Company   **Owner/Manager**
Established and ran a commercial marketing and bulk mail distribution company. Operations included manufacturing, design, order entry, production and customer service.

1/81–4/98: IBM
9/95–4/98   **Project Manager**
Project management of global teams consisting of 60-70 professionals, integrating external and internal problem and change management databases and processes into the IBM systems. Provided pre-contract evaluation and integrated solutions of IS service proposals. Evaluated cost effacement methods for management. Provided education to internal and external customers for process changes using database services.

- Customer pre-contract engagements: Developed proposals assuring the integrity and completeness of the contract information. Worked with global team, evaluating current IT processes and analyzing current processes to determine potential efficiencies. Assured every issue was addressed so as not to impact the customer. Provided and designed education sessions based on the integrated solution. Reported to management and customer details of the proposal and recommendations enabling the contract to meet all guidelines and expectations. Evaluated I/T contracts for the following industries: Banking, Stock and Insurance and Utilities.
- Database Migration Projects: Gathered requirements with creatively integrating solutions to migrate existing problem and change management databases into IBM. Team Leader of 60 database, networking, programming, helpdesk, operations, security, and project office professionals. Projects required the integration of education and communications to the customers and management. Resolved all issues and documented new and updated procedures. Provided security of customer information. Customers included internal IBM accounts along with accounts in Health Care, Banking, Government, and Utilities.

3/93–9/95   **Availability Manager / Crisis Manager**
Maintained high availability and customer satisfaction for over 25 large systems remotely. Provided crisis and situation management for problems, assuring best resources worked toward solid and timely solutions.
- Reported details of the outages and final solution to customers and management, ensuring resolution of all problems.
- Evaluated systems to ensure availability of best and latest software.
- Monitored system performance.
- Provided migration support while bringing new systems under control of IBM processes, assuring that proper support was provided throughout the process and beyond.
- Evaluated all changes made to systems.
- Planned, scheduled, resolved pre-reqs, and communicated changes, assuring resolution of all conflicts, necessary changes prior to implementation.
- Assured fulfillment of contract commitments.
- Planned and executed migration of systems from Minnesota to New York, minimizing impact to the customer. Systems responsible for software and hardware development, test, as well as customer help functions for the AS/400 product line.
- Interacted with Account Team, Customers, Programming Teams, Hardware Planning, Security and Facilities. Project completed ahead of schedule with minimal customer impact.

> WHY SO MUCH DETAIL? BECAUSE A POTENTIAL CLIENT WANTS TO KNOW WHAT YOU'VE DONE FOR OTHER CLIENTS BEFORE ENTRUSTING YOU WITH KEY RESPONSIBILITIES.

Grant S. Livermore

541 Oakwood Ave.
Roselle Park, NJ 07204
GSLivermor@aol.com

> A STRONG, YET CURIOUSLY
> UNDERSTATED SUMMARY

SUMMARY

A highly motivated and seasoned professional with excellent communications skills, proven leadership abilities and extensive experience in Information Technology.

ACCOMPLISHMENTS/CAREER HISTORY

4/2000–Present   PROJECT AND RESOURCE MANAGEMENT   **Senior Project Manager**

- Manage software development and installation projects for the Research Division of a large New Jersey-based pharmaceutical company: develop and manage project plans and resources.
- Managed I/T Infrastructure components of projects, developed and managed project plans and infrastructure resources.
- Managed Information Services Team: mentored Project Managers in the process and techniques of Project Management, managed testing of Intranet Portal application.

1/2000–4/2000   **Program Director**

Implemented Program Management Office (PMO) for major insurance company for e-commerce, new technology conversion and Internet development projects. Mentored project leads, developed project plans for 10 projects and reporting status.

11/1998–11/1999   **Project Manager**

Managed a Y2K (Year 2000) project for a division of a large New Jersey based pharmaceutical company: managed remediation of client-server applications and infrastructure, auditing of CRO for risk evaluation, overseeing validation protocol development, and development of contingency planning.

10/1997–10/1998   **Consulting Manager**

- Directed Southern Tier New York office of a national consulting firm: supervised fifty consultants, maintained account responsibility for eight accounts.
- Managed Y2K (Year 2000) project for major New York Insurance company in: supervised twenty consultants, mentored junior Project Managers, led Team Building effort and reorganization into software factory model.
- Managed a Phase I Y2K (Year 2000) inventory delivery engagement for Hospital organization. Recruited and mentored Project Manager for subsequent phases II/III.

6/1996–9/1997   **Principal Consultant**

Developed business applications solutions for Manufacturing company. Utilized MS/Access and interfaced with ORACLE databases in TCP/IP, Windows NT networked environment. Led projects for Corporate I/T including client/server, EDI, MS/Exchange and Windows NT rollout.

Chronological

Grant S. Livermore

11/1994-6/1996   **Consultant**

Authored Strategic I/T plans for several local governments and manufacturing business units.
- Formulated full disaster recovery plan for a Town Government with mixed hardware platform.
- Implemented Novell Netware 4.x Local Area Network, integrating an AS/400 over an Ethernet backbone.
- Installed several Windows95 workstations, connecting into the LAN.
- Designed and administered multi-user relational database application incorporating automatic backup procedures.

RESPONSIBILITIES AND RESULTS IN DIFFERENT ENVIRONMENTS

1990–1994   **Director of Information Services–Government Entity**

Directed I/T organization, including a full data center and a staff of twenty in a successful, 24 by 7 operation.
- Led several high profile projects including Image processing, Computer-Aided Dispatch, Geographic Information Systems, Financial/Human Resource System including re-engineering, multiple platforms and client/server technology.
- Planned and updated data center, including new raised floor, HVAC, UPS, early fire detection, security, implementing new computing platform and accompanying operating systems, and high speed data communications network.
- Developed full disaster recovery plan, including use of hot-site facility running multiple drills.
- Enhanced I/T revenue process to totally support $2M operating budget, while employing TQM principles, including service level agreements and customer satisfaction surveys.
- Served as President of the NYS Information Technology Directors Association, assisting in conference planning, NYS legislation lobbying, Vision/2000 projects and seminars.

PROFESSIONAL SEMINARS

ONGOING EDUCATION AND INTEREST

Project Management   Year 2000 Compliance
Quality Training for Managers   PMI: PM for the Experienced Professional
Managerial Leadership   Applied 21 CFR Part 11 training
Multiple technical courses in Operating systems and networking

EDUCATION

Bachelor of Science: Albany University, Albany NY–Mathematics/Computer Science

Resume Example #32: Consulting
A nontechnical consultant displays years of experience and achievement.

Arthur D. Rosenberg

PROJECT LEADER / ANALYST / TRAINER / DOCUMENTATION SPECIALIST

Business Analysis/Testing/Project Management
Training for End Users and Trainers
User/Instructional Manuals

> THESE TOPICS CAN BE
> REARRANGED AS NEEDED

SERVICE:

> A CLEAR SUMMARY
> OF SERVICES

Team and project management; business analysis and testing; assessment and creation of innovative documentation and training materials, requirements documents, RFP's and proposals. Applications include a wide range of financial services, insurance, telecommunications, sales & marketing, publishing and human resources.

SOFTWARE: Most major Windows/DOS word processors, spreadsheets, and flow chart tools.

PROFESSIONAL ACCOMPLISHMENTS

> THIS REPETITIVE FORMAT IS PREFERRED BY
> MANY CONSULTING FIRMS AND AGENCIES

- For Schering-Plough: 3/02–Present

    Analyze and create business requirements, scoping, validation, and compliance-related materials for the research institute of a leading pharmaceuticals company. Review source documents, interview user groups, coordinate with analysts, write documents.

- For Prudential Securities: 3/01–2/02

    Coordinated with business and programming departments on successful conversion of old (insurance division) client services package to correspond to securities-based system. Wrote detailed business requirements and specifications, participated in sign-off testing. Components included fees, statements, related internal and external on-line systems, money funds & sweeps, service & operations (voice response unit, trade desk, service center), notification to internal departments and external vendors.

- For Paine Webber (Business Systems Division): 4/00–2/01

    Managed two interrelated projects for Wealth Management Group:

    1. Collaborated with other department to create automated Presentation Builder for over 10,000 brokers. Wrote business requirements, negotiated modifications for in-house deliverable, then wrote requirements for Phase 2.
    2. Researched products and services, performed proof-of-concept, and wrote business requirements for off-site development of Collaborative Workspace for High New Worth group. Scheduled and conducted presentations by selected vendors, created comparative technology and time/cost grids, recommended vendor, and successfully organized selection and project initiation processes.

Also contributed to multi-lingual communications flow with UBS following acquisition.

- For Enterprise Technology Corporation: 10/99–4/00

    Documented customized trading and portfolio management systems for high-profile clients of financial consulting and software development corporation. Also wrote promotional project descriptions and contributed to creation of new company WEB-site.

- For AT&T: 8/99–10/99

    Wrote business requirements for Oracle-based on-line filtering system used to enable massive customer account migration.

Combined

- For Scholastic Books: 4/99–8/99

    Researched and wrote business requirements document, design specifications, and presentation materials for major WEB-based ordering system; member of team gathering and prioritizing user requirements. Organized and created applications development documents for Cybase application and related design documents.
- For AT&T: 10/98–3/99

    Created interactive training tutorial for on-line filtering system used to enable massive customer account migration.
- For Citicorp: 2/98–9/98

    Documented several highly visible software systems; defined and upgraded documentation standards; wrote QA, testing, and GUI development standards.
- For AT&T: 11/95–1/99

    Member of project development and requirements team for major financial system. Documented and trained on-line and Web-based financial, sales, customer evaluation systems, and Y2K requirements. Wrote GUI, QA, and testing standards. Delivered on-line help and tutorials. Designed and conducted user training classes.
- For Teleport Communications Group (TCG): 4/94–10/95

    Documented several highly visible software systems; defined and upgraded documentation standards; wrote QA, testing, and GUI development standards; introduced on-line help documentation; edited department status reports.
- For Cubic Automatic Revenue Collection Group: 7/93–3/94

    Tested and documented results for new fare collection system.
- For Deutsche Bank: 6/93

    Created prototype for documentation of international (multilingual) trading system.
- For MTV/Viacom: 1/93–5/93

    Hired and managed team of 8 consultants in testing, documenting, and training customized JD Edwards/Synon A/R installation. Organized testing and training schedules throughout system implementation. Member of project management team.
- For United Parcel Service: 4/92–12/92

    Analyzed and rewrote portion of customized methodology, based on Catalyst (CSC Partners) and Method/1 (Arthur Anderson).

CLIENT LIST

Managed multiple projects; analyzed and documented a wide variety of applications; conducted classes and training seminars in PC hardware and software, mainframe applications and methodology to clerical, managerial and technical staff at:

The Port Authority of New York and New Jersey	AT&T
Cubic Automatic Revenue Collection Group	Citibank
Morgan Guaranty and Trust Company	Scholastic
Teleport Communications Group (TCG)	Viacom / MTV
American International Group (AIG)	Paine Webber
Enterprise Technology Corporation	Deutsche Bank
University of Stockholm (Sweden)	Schering-Plough
New York City Housing Authority	Purolator Courier
Lucent Technologies / Bell Labs	Delmar Publishers

A CREATIVE WAY TO LIST
OVER **30** CLIENTS

New York City Transit Authority	Union College (NJ)
Marine Computer Enterprises	John Wiley & Sons
United Parcel Service (UPS)	Marsh & McLennan
US Department of Education	Paramount Pictures
Paladyne Software Systems	Information Science
McGraw-Hill Book Company	Berlitz School (Paris)

MORE FOOD FOR THOUGHT, BUT DEFINITELY RELATED TO THE EARLIER DESCRIPTIONS

RELATED ACHIEVEMENTS

- Directed marketing activities for two international publishers of technical and educational materials.
- Supervised multinational staff at United Nations agency in Geneva, Switzerland.
- Published and marketed college textbooks and related educational materials.
- Translator / interpreter for Organizing Committee of 1968 Grenoble Olympic Games.

EDUCATION

MA, English, French–University of Grenoble, France
BA, Psychology–University of California at Los Angeles

PROFESSIONAL ASSOCIATIONS

ICCA–Independent Computer Consultants Association   PROFESSIONAL CREDENTIALS
The Authors Guild, The Authors League

FOREIGN LANGUAGES

French, Spanish, German, Italian, Dutch, Swedish

COMMUNITY SERVICE

Provide career-related seminars and training classes to a number of minority and professional groups
and organizations.

PUBLICATIONS   WRITERS, RESEARCHERS, AND ACADEMICS ARE USUALLY EXPECTED TO HAVE SOME PUBLICATIONS

BOOKS

THE REQUIREMENTS OF PROGRAMMING, the first section (four chapters) of the book, *ACE THE TECHNICAL JOB.*
2000, McGraw-Hill Book Co., New York
PREPARING FOR A SUCCESSFUL INTERVIEW, initial chapter in the book, *ACE THE TECHNICAL INTERVIEW.*
2000 [4th edition], McGraw-Hill Book Co., New York
CAREER BUSTERS–22 WAYS PEOPLE MESS UP THEIR CAREERS AND HOW TO AVOID THEM
1997, McGraw-Hill Book Co.
THE RESUME HANDBOOK
2003 [4th edition], Adams Media Corp., Avon, MA.
MANIPULATIVE MEMOS–CONTROL YOUR CAREER THROUGH THE MEDIUM OF THE MEMO
1994, Tenspeed Press, Berkeley, CA.
CHESS FOR CHILDREN AND THE YOUNG AT HEART
1977, Atheneum, New York

Combined

ARTICLES

> **CONTROL YOUR CAREER WITH MEMOS**
> *National Business Employment Weekly* (Published by the *Wall Street Journal)*, May, 1995.
> **KEEPING YOUR JOB IN A TECHNICAL ENVIRONMENT**
> *National Business Employment Weekly*, February, 1987.
> **HOW TO BECOME A COMPUTER CONSULTANT**
> *National Business Employment Weekly*, September, 1986.
> **MAKING THE TRANSITION TO A TECHNICAL CAREER**
> *National Business Employment Weekly,* June, 1985.
> **RESUME STRATEGY**
> *National Business Employment Weekly* (3-article series), June, 1985.
> **HABIT UN-FORMING** *(interviewing techniques)*
> *National Business Employment Weekly*, March, 1982.

OVERVIEW

Documentation	**Business Analysis**	**Training**
Assess scope, objective, & target of deliverables.	Define and write business requirements.	Assess scope, objective, & target of objectives.
scope: - what to include - estimated time & resources	Incorporate company standards and procedures.	**scope:** - what to cover - creation of training materials - estimated time & resources
objective: - user or technical manual - system or functional	Schedule development: - if onsite, coordinate deliverables / milestones - if offsite, conduct proof-of-concept, assist in vendor selection, assess progress	**objective:** - overview - functional knowledge
audience: - in house business users - external client users - technical staff		**audience:** - in house business users - external client users - technical staff - trainers
Write manual: - obtain feedback through delivery of milestones - include realistic examples	Create & apply user acceptance testing scenarios.	Write training guide based (if possible) on user guide.
	Schedule system testing, bug reviews, fixes.	Schedule & conduct training classes.
	Coordinate rollout, training, & documentation.	
	Determine need for system & functional upgrades.	

> AN ORIGINAL ATTEMPT TO DISTINGUISH BETWEEN SEVERAL DIFFERENT SPECIALTIES AND SERVICES.

CHAPTER FIVE

The Five Worst Resumes We've Ever Seen

If a good resume is a work of art, a bad resume is an envoy of self-destruction.

Included in this chapter are five of the worst resumes we've ever seen, selected from among thousands of misguided attempts at interesting potential employers. That they fail is obvious. We shall briefly point out some of their most blatant flaws, and we will show you how three of them could have been successfully rewritten.

Worst Resume #1: Vinny Vaguely

RESUME   Vinny Vaguely

PERSONAL: Birth Date: February 25, 1979. Single. Excellent health.
                     Willing to travel and/or relocate.

EDUCATION: B.S. in Business Administration, Central Michigan
                     University, with a major in finance, 24 credit hours;
                     additional concentration in marketing and economics.
                     Overall GPA 3.1. Date of graduation, May 7, 1993.

EXTRA-   Marketing Association, 1997, 1998, 2000
CURRICULAR   Finance Club, 1998–2001
ACTIVITIES: Student Advisory Council, 1998–2001
                     Theta Chi Fraternity–Secretary, 1994–1998
                     Rush Chairman, 1998–1999

HOBBIES and   Sports (golf, bowling, softball, basketball); leisure
INTERESTS: reading, and music.

WORK   1995–Warehouseman for Leaseway of Westland, MI
EXPERIENCE: 1996–Warehouseman for Leaseway of Westland, MI
                     1997–Warehouseman for Leaseway of Westland, MI
                     1998–Temporary Welding Inspector–Ford Motor
                     Company (after being laid off, painted exteriors of homes)

ADDRESS: Home: 66666 Fox Glen
                     Farmington Hills, MI 48018
                     Phone: 313-666-0606, 313-666-0607

COMMENTS: I feel that I am a dependable, personable, and hard working
                     individual who could be an asset to your business.

Name: Vinny Vaguely

Vinny Vaguely's vitae could (and maybe should) have been written on a 3" x 5" index card, the ideal size for recipes and other nonessentials. Although Vaguely seems to feel that he'd be an asset to our business, he has given us precious little data to support this optimistic view.

Now let's take a look at what Vincent Vaguely *did* include:

- *Resume*: We can guess what it was intended to be, so the label is superfluous.
- *Personal*: This information is unnecessary. If the writer insists on including it, he should have placed it at the very end.
- *Education*: Adequate, but poorly presented.
- *Extracurricular Activities*: Okay, but "Related Activities" might appear more grown-up.
- *Interests, Hobbies*: Who cares?
- *Work Experience*: Should list last job first. The same job need not be listed more than once. No mention is made of job responsibilities or accomplishments.
- *Address*: We finally discover where Vinny Vaguely lives. Of course, the address belongs up at the top.
- *Comments*: Unsubstantiated and unconvincing.

Worst Resume #2: Charles "Chucky" Confuser

Charles "Chucky" Confuser   Telex: Smartashell
Easy Street
Big Town, NJ 07990

Statement of Position
As of July 20, 2001

"U" are current unit valuations of relative worth to investor.

ASSETS
CURRENT ASSETS
Abilities Derived Through Current Major Classes
    Technical Capabilities   U   55
    Spirit of competition
      (less allowance for cooperation)   90
    Communicative capacity   90
    Background in business courses   **100**
    Units from current major classes   335
    Leadership/Decision Making Ability   **125**
      TOTAL CURRENT ASSETS   460
    Health and Physical Attributes   100
    Former Education   75
    Determination, Self-Confidence, and Self-Support
      (net of realization of dependence on others)   125
    Goodwill and Intangibles   **100**
TOTAL ASSETS   U   860

LIABILITIES AND STOCKHOLDERS EQUITY
CURRENT LIABILITIES
    Amount Due Others for Maintenance of Interest and Self-Development U   235
    Amount Due Work Experience   **115**
      TOTAL CURRENT LIABILITIES   350
    Long Term Debt to Supporters of Current Position   140
    Debt related to Mark 12:17   **110**
    TOTAL LIABILITIES   600
    STOCKHOLDERS EQUITY
    Common Stock   55
    Retained Earnings (to facilitate future development)   **210**
    TOTAL LIABILITIES AND STOCKHOLDERS EQUITY   U   860

Name: Charles "Chuck" Confuser

Believe it or not, such resumes as this actually *do* turn up from time to time. Chucky has obviously confused numerical facility with imagination and cleverness; a potential employer would not. This is not to say that innovation and creativity are negative ingredients in resume-writing perforce. But they must be applied judiciously and intelligently so as to complement, not dominate, important and clearly-organized information.

This document not only is *not* a resume, it doesn't come close to fulfilling the *purpose* of a resume. Even if someone took the trouble to try and figure out the "formula" (bear in mind the other stack of resumes waiting on the interviewer's desk), it provides no comprehensible basis on which to evaluate the aspirant's experience or abilities.

The lesson here is that a resume should provide its readers with relevant information; it shouldn't test their patience.

If all of this were not enough, the use of a nickname is another "no-no."

Worst Resume #3: Eleanora Unsura

Eleanora Unsura
1404 Moore Ave.
Lincoln, MO 65438
(417) 555-1174
Social Sec. No. 390-92-6649

Level of Education: High School Harper Woods High School 4 years
Business School Hallmark Business Machines Institute 9 months
Course of study Computer Programming
Specialization Cobol & RPGII Languages
Career Objective To Work Hard and become a good Programmer
Possible Salary $15,000 to $20,000 a year
Employment Experience:
Present Employer Whall Security Corp.
Job Title Security Officer.
Date of Employment 12/27/99. Current Salary of $4.25 an hour
Job Responsibility To Take care of clients property from Fire of Theft
Previous Employer Little Caecars Inc.
Job Title Store manager & pizza maker
Dates of Employment March, 1990 to November, 1991 Salary $180 a week.
Job Responsibility To make pizzas when busy and to do daily paper work.
Personal References: Billy and Jane Smith, 1403 Moore Ave. (across the street).

Truly Yours

Eleanora Unsura

Name: Eleanora Unsura

What's wrong with this little monstrosity? Almost everything! The major flaws are that it is grammatically abhorrent, poorly punctuated, full of misspellings, and unpleasing to the eye. It goes on to flout, destroy, or ignore virtually all of the fundamental rules of writing a successful resume.

To mention just a few specifics, salaries (past, present, and requested) should *never* appear upon a resume. If you insist on listing references, at least spell the name of your employer correctly. Finally, Eleanora's resume doesn't give the interviewer a chance to think about her background. There is no open space; relevancies and irrelevancies are intermingled, and it is completely lacking in structure.

Ms. Unsura gives us no idea of what she may have to offer a potential employer. She would be well-advised to solicit help in organizing and writing a resume with purpose and technique.

On the following page, we offer an alternative.

Eleanora Unsura

1404 Moore Avenue   (417) 555-1174
Lincoln, Missouri 65438

OBJECTIVE: A programming position allowing for professional skill
                    development, multiple applications, and potential for career growth.

EMPLOYMENT   Whall Security Corporation–Security Officer
HISTORY: Provide security service to a variety of business clients—hospitals to
1999–Present   manufacturing concerns.

                    • Discovered electrical fire in early stages while on patrol at
                      Parkcrest Hospital, resulting in quick and easy smothering of fire
                      and saving potential loss of costly research equipment.
                    • Maintained perfect attendance record while employed at Whall,
                      despite working at least thirty hours/week and completing
                      coursework at Hallmark.
                    • "Employee of the Month"—Recipient seven times.

1990–1999   Little Caesar's Incorporated—Store Manager
                    Managed $515,000 annual receipt, seven-employee carry-out
                    restaurant.

                    • Reduced losses from incorrectly filled orders by redesigning order
                      form. This resulted in a 55% drop in losses.
                    • Appointed manager at age seventeen and while still a senior in
                      high school.

EDUCATION: Hallmark Business Machines Institute—2000.
                    Completed nine-month computer programming program with a
                    proficiency score on final testing of 92%.

                    Harper Woods H.S., 1999. Graduated within College Preparatory
                    Curriculum.

ACTIVE
INTERESTS: Home computers, computer technical journals.

Yes, this is the same Eleanora Unsura who authored the previous interviewer's nightmare. With some careful thought awarded her achievements, a newfound respect for the English language, some carefully chosen action verbs, and a logical format, Eleanora's resume has made a Pygmalion-like transition.

Worst Resume #4: I. M. Brusk

RESUME

I.M. Brusk
123 S. Adams
Correl, California 91106
(213) 000-0000

Department of Geography
California State University
80 State College Avenue
Fullerton, California 91106
(213) 000-0001

EDUCATION

1991	School of Business Administration & Economics California State University–Fullerton M.B.A.
1989–1993	Economic Geography Option U.C. Berkeley Ph.D.
1986–1989	Geography, Major–Economics, Minor B.A. University of Bristol (England) Special Honors

WORK EXPERIENCE

1997–present	Associate Professor Department of Geography California State University–Fullerton
1993–1997	Assistant Professor Department of Geography California State University–Fullerton
1992–1993	Instructor Department of Economics University of San Francisco

CONSULTING

1999–Present	Urban Econometrics Co., Fullerton, Ca.
1999–2002	Market Profiles, Inc., Tustin, Ca.
1999	Orange County Forecast and Analysis Center

AWARDS, HONORS

1990–1991	James P. Sutton Fellowship, U.C. Berkeley
1989–1990	Thomas and Elizabeth Williams Scholarship, Glamorgan City Council
1986–1989	Special Honors, University of Bristol

Name: I.M. Brusk

What a pity to portray such an impressive record of academic excellence in such an unimpressive fashion.

This resume tells us that I.M. Brusk has earned an M.B.A., a Ph.D., and special honors. We can further deduce, with careful study, that the individual was promoted from Assistant to Associate Professor.

The rest is speculation. Has this seemingly intelligent person published? What courses and seminars has he taught? What are his academic and scientific specialties? What was the nature of his consulting? Has he any noteworthy research in progress? What, if any, are his goals? Why, we don't even know if he is, in fact, a *he* or a *she*.

Presumably, Professor Brusk is looking for a highly specialized position. However, there are other qualified people out there with Ph.D.s and honors of their own in competition. Given similar academic credentials, those whose resumes present them in a more interesting light are likelier to win the interview.

Our advice to I.M. Brusk is to rewrite this resume with the elements we've outlined in *The Resume Handbook*. It might look something like the one on the following page.

ISABELLA M. BRUSK

123 South Adams
Correl, California 91106

Residence: (213) 000-0000
Work: (213) 000-0000

EXPERIENCE

1991–Current

California State University–Fullerton, Associate Professor, Department of Geography. Responsible for curriculum development for entire department covering 3,700 students annually. Personally direct ten department classes each year, including newly designed class entitled "Changing Weather Patterns–Dawn of a New Age."

- Co-authored "Economic Cycle Influences of Changing Political Boundaries," a highly acclaimed series of articles appearing in July–October 2000 issues of the *Research Economist*.

Selected as:

- Member of Governor's Council on Earthquake Readiness, a sixteen-member task force of business, academic, and government people assessing current state readiness regarding safety, economic disruption and proposed construction considerations. Youngest member of panel.
- Rated 96.4 out of 100 by nearly 750 students attending my classes during 1997–2000. "90" is considered "outstanding."
- Developed and tested computer model identifying economic trends (i.e., unemployment rates, median incomes, others) caused by changing populations. This was accomplished during a consulting assignment with Urban Econometrics, Fullerton, CA.
- Conceived, designed and sold predictive voting model that pinpoints political voting trends utilizing demographics rather than polling. This predictive model has accurately predicted twenty-seven out of twenty-nine county races in 1980–2000.

1990–1991

University of San Francisco, Instructor–Department of Economics. Responsible for leading one senior-level undergrad and two graduate-level Microeconomics classes involving 120+ students.

- Developed instructional curriculum for sixty-hour class entitled "Economic Patterns and Their Historical Perspectives."

PROFESSIONAL ASSOCIATION
American Association of Geographers

page 2

LANGUAGES
Welsh, French

PUBLICATIONS

1. *Hydrological Implications of Geothermal Developments in the Imperial Valley of Southern California*
    with G. George, R.H. Foster, and D.K. Todd
    Sea Water Conversion Laboratory, UCB, Richmond, November, 1992.

2. *1988 Population Estimate*
    with G. George and G. Britton
    Report on the Status of Orange County, 1995. Working Document No. 1, Forecast and Analysis Center, Orange County, CA.

3. *The Frequency of Social Contracts within a Time-Space Framework.*
    with G. George
    Submitted for publication.

PROFESSIONAL PAPERS

1. *Intra-Urban Interaction and Time-Space Budgets*
    with G. George, D. Shimarua, and P. Barry
    Association of American Geographers, New Orleans, 1999.

2. *The Soviet Concept of Optimal City Size*
    with G. George and C. Zumbrunnen
    Association of American Geographers, New Orleans, 1999.

EDUCATION

- Ph.D.-University of California at Berkeley, 1993.
  Economic Geography Option
- M.B.A.–California State University-Fullerton, 1991.
- B.A.-University of Bristol (England), 1989.
- Geography Major; Economics Minor. Graduated with honors.

We discover not only that Dr. Brusk is a she, we also gain a wealth of important information omitted from her initial resume. We learn about her areas of expertise, that she has published extensively, and that she's popular with her students. Dr. Brusk, we find, has been appointed to a government panel; she is familiar with state-of-the-art techniques (computer modeling), and has had consulting positions with private firms (no "bookish academic," this Dr. Brusk). Without any exaggeration, her limp and lifeless resume has morphed into one that will demand its share of recognition in a fiercely competitive market.

Worst Resume #5: Bart Bonehead

RESUME
OF
BART BONEHEAD

RESIDENCE:
808 Hopkins Drive East
Windsor, Ontario

OFFICE:
Graduate School of Business
Administration
The University of Windsor
Windsor, Ontario

PROFESSIONAL EXPERIENCE:

1998 to Present	The University of Windsor, Windsor, Ontario
2000 to Present	Director of Placement, Graduate School of Business Administration
1988 to 1990	Director, BBA Internship Program, Dearborn, Michigan Campus
1994 to 1998	Substitute Teacher Windsor Public Schools Windsor, Ontario
1990 to 1994	Training Manager Hespin & Marquette Windsor, Ontario
1986 to 1990	Home Economics Teacher Weaton Public Schools Weaton, Ontario

EDUCATION:

University of Windsor, Windsor, Ontario; Master of Business Administration, 1992. Major: Industrial Relations

University of Buffalo, Buffalo, New York; Bachelor of Science, 1990. Major: Secondary Education

EXCELLENT REFERENCES AVAILABLE UPON REQUEST

Name: Bart Bonehead

This resume is probably the most frequent, and thus typical, form of resume failure we've encountered. At first glance, it may not seem so bad. In fact, you may be saying, "Gee, that looks like my resume!"

Indeed, Bonehead's offering is not as obviously awful as some of the preceding examples of bad resumes. Its failure is more subtle and insidious, which is why we consider it more dangerous than the others. The problem isn't what you see, but rather what you don't.

At second glance, this sad excuse for a resume might be better suited to a footnote to Bart's career—it offers little more than the stuff of which memories are made. What, if anything, has he accomplished in his profession? Has he met with any noteworthy success? There must be *something* he has done over the years to interest a potential employer, but we can't find it here.

Other than where Bonehead has been, and when, this document provides job titles, identifies itself as his resume, and promises good references to anyone who might be interested. Fortunately, we know Bart well enough to help him out of his predicament, and so we took the time to rewrite his notes into a solid resume. They hardly appear to describe the same person.

Worst Resume #5 Alternative: Bartholomew X. Bonehead

Bartholomew X. Bonehead

808 Hopkins Drive East
Windsor, Ontario 74R 01S

Residence (519) 101-0001
Business (519) 010-1000

PROFESSIONAL OBJECTIVE

Attainment of a managerial level position as a Programs Director, Project Manager, or Section Head within a major university where my array of administrative, analytic, planning, and leadership skills can be fully utilized.

EDUCATION

M.B.A., University of Windsor, Windsor, Ontario—1982.
Concentration in Industrial Relations. B.A., University of Buffalo, Buffalo, New York–1990. Major in Secondary Education.

SIGNIFICANT EXPERIENCE

MANAGERIAL–Successfully headed twelve-member, $540,000 annual budget placement function; increased enrollments 1147 over last four years at a 9000-student university.

SYSTEMS DEVELOPMENT–Conceptualized and implemented computerized records system projected to save $175,000 in administrative expenses over next three years.

FUNDS DEVELOPMENT–During two-year assignment as BBA Internship Program Director: established 359 successful corporate relationships totaling 577 students, resulting in additional bottom-line impact to university of $205,000.

PROGRAM DESIGN–Originated and initiated Student Enrollment Campaign involving promotional literature, student contacts at high schools and junior colleges, and direct mail: resulted in increase in enrollment during 1997 of 660 over 1996.

TRAINING DESIGN–Designed Comprehensive Management Program affecting 275 individuals covering all phases of management from planning to controlling for major Canadian retailer.

TEACHING EXCELLENCE–Runner-up two years in row (1982-83) as Teacher of the Year in a school district with 150 high school teachers.

POSITIONS

1988–Present   Director of Placement, University of Windsor, Windsor, Ontario (2000–Present).

Director of BBA Internship Programs, University of Windsor (1998–2000).

1994–1998   Substitute Teacher, Windsor Public Schools.

1990–1994   Training Manager, Hespin & Marquette Ltd., Windsor, Ontario.

1986–1990   Home Economics Teacher, Weaton Public Schools, Weaton, Ontario

Unlike Bart's first attempt, his rewritten resume shows that his flatly stated job titles were accompanied by significant managerial, fiscal, teaching, and operational responsibilities. In the first resume, his job progression seems sketchy and undefined. The improved version informs us of a logical progression toward the position he is seeking. Bart's new resume is an interview-getter.

• • • •

Conclusion

We've done our best to convince you that even losing resumes can be transformed into winners. All you need are several hours of honest reflection (armed, of course, with your "resume tools"), an awareness of how your background can make you valuable to a potential employer, and a quick review of the basic resume guidelines outlined in chapter two. The rest is personal: choosing the format, typestyle, and layout that you feel best suits your background, and avoiding the pitfalls of poor resume writing.

Except for the brief final chapter on resume layout and design, this is our final word on successful resumes. The examples we have given you will, we hope, provide the tools you need for your own, unique profile.

However, this is not the end of *The Resume Handbook*. In the following chapters, we'll talk about design and layout, and then focus on the two essential resume companions: the cover letter, and the personal sales (or broadcast) letter. After that, we introduce our brand-new chapters on networking and other job-getting and changing activities.

CHAPTER SIX
Presentation

It's no less important that your resume be pleasing to the eye than for it to clearly present the facts of your job history. This chapter will serve as a brief guide to structuring a resume that is graphically appealing and complementary to your background.

Typeface

The first thing to consider is your choice of typeface. You want your resume to stand out, not compete with wedding or funeral announcements. Our advice is that you stick to a simple, clean typeface like Arial, Times Roman, or Helvetica. They are our choice because of their simplicity of design and clarity.

Another trap to avoid is combining different typeface styles (like Times Roman and Helvetica). Each of these typefaces offers a variety of light, italic, and bold that can be used to produce an attractive visual effect.

Length

Debate among the "experts" continues as to whether resumes must be limited to a single page. Our take on this reverts to common sense:

- If your work experience is limited, i.e., you are a recent graduate or have only held one or two jobs, there is probably no reason for your resume to exceed a single page.
- If you can reasonably limit your resume to one page, do so.
- If you have held a number of positions and cannot describe your accomplishments and responsibilities on one page, then two pages are certainly acceptable. However, you do not need to provide detailed descriptions of jobs that date back more than eight or ten years, unless they add something significant to your experience and qualifications. Be sure to emphasize your most recent experience.
- Attachments, such as additional pages of publications (for writers, researchers, and academics), are appropriate.
- *Exception*: Consulting resumes are expected to include all relevant experience, even if they extend to multiple pages.

Layout

When you design your resume, bear in mind that open spaces make it easier to read. Avoid cramming your page(s) with heavy masses of print. For example, compare Eleanora Unsura's two resumes in Chapter Five.

Paper

Standard office stationery is the safe choice of paper on which to print your resume and cover letter, although a quality paper stock may improve the overall effect. Slightly off-white paper is acceptable, but beware of using pastels or darker colors, which look unprofessional.

Print as many originals of your resume as you need on attractive, letter-quality paper. Never send photocopies of your resume to a potential employer. They're okay for friends or employment agencies, but not the employer with whom you want to win an interview.

Another point is that the resume you mail may be photocopied by a personnel department, and subsequently passed along to other members of their firm. Copies made from copies can lose readability. In an emergency, some professionally maintained office photocopiers may do a good job, but we think it's better to avoid such emergencies by always having "perfect" copies of your resume on hand.

Accuracy

A final word: Proofread your resume at every step in the process. Get a knowledgeable friend or colleague to help. Mistakes on resumes are embarrassing, unacceptable, and potentially disastrous. No matter how much you may pay to have your resume created, you're the one who loses if it isn't right. So be meticulous and don't settle for less than the very best.

By way of example, look at the before and after versions of E. N. Trepreneurial's resume.

Before:

E. N. Trepreneurial

3000 High Expectations Way
Southfield, MI 48075
810-555-1122

CAREER SUMMARY

Twenty-three years of experience as an owner/executive of various types of companies including high technology, real estate services, and manufacturing.

EXPERIENCE

ENTREPRENEURIAL VENTURES, INC./COMMUNITY OF HOMES STUDIO, President and Founder
Entrepreneurial Ventures is a consulting company specializing in sales generation and growth (including turnarounds) locally, nationally, and internationally. Company manages all phases of marketing and management of approved plans. Client companies are start-ups through large international corporations that are in need of immediate attention and/or growth.

Company also arranges Venture Capital, equity financing, debt financing, mortgage, lease, etc. financing through Venture Strategies, Inc., an investment banking firm in Southfield, Michigan. Entrepreneurial Ventures assists automotive, manufacturing, real estate/building, computer/software, high tech, health care, robotics, electronics, publishing, consumer products, and service companies.

Community Of Homes Studio was a company financed and managed by Entrepreneurial Ventures. Community Of Homes Studio had the largest indoor showroom of modular homes in the U.S. (93,000 sq. ft.). Featured ten homes that were landscaped and decorated in a village-like atmosphere with pond and waterfalls. Facility also had displays, mortgage companies, insurance companies, employment agencies, credit counselors, builders and developers, a restaurant, and day care. Activities involved housing financing as well as community affairs and parties. First six weeks generated 1,643 mortgage-approved buyers.

ENTREPRENEURIAL COMMUNITY HOMES, President and Founder

Manufactured housing company that erected homes in subdivisions and scattered lots in eleven counties near metro Detroit.

ENVIRA CORPORATION, President and CEO

Research and Development Company specializing in aerospace remote sensing and image processing. Responsibilities included commercializing scientific developments with oil and gas companies, Department of Defense, medical institutions and other governmental agencies.

ZANADU INTERNATIONAL, Executive Vice-President and Co-Founder

Washington company that provided electrical and electronic components to the lighting industry. Responsibilities included strategic/business planning and day-to-day general management with over 500 people in twenty-four offices in the United States and London, England. Growth from start-up to $78 million in sales in three-year period.

COMMUNITY CONSTRUCTION COMPANY, President and Founder

Home building company that constructed over four hundred residential homes, numerous condominiums, and several light industrial buildings in Metropolitan Seattle. Responsibility was overall management.

VILLAGE MANAGEMENT CORPORATION, President and Co-Founder

First condominium property management company in Washington.
Customers included Hanson Homes, Hobbs & Cintas, Lewis & Lewis, and Allison Development. Managed maintenance, insurance, banking, repairs, construction, and developer relations. Company managed over 6,000 units and expanded operations to include condominium sales.

BENNINGTON INTERNATIONAL INC., Vice President

Marketing and Sales Manager, Ohio Division. Managed three used home sales offices consisting of over one hundred sales and administrative personnel. Also, was responsible for Bennington - New Town, a 61,000-acre development of residential and commercial property in Lester Township, Illinois. Responsibilities included planning, land development, municipal relations, serving on homeowners association, antique village (thirty-acre amusement and historical village), marketing, and supervising commercial and residential sales. Also managed two other land developments in the Bloomington area.

Sales/Marketing Manager, Bennington - New Town. Responsible for all new home building activities as well as commercial land sales. Duties included contracts, pricing, floor plans, home closings, builder relations, warranty, broker relations, advertising and promotion, and sales staff management.

After:

Elias N. Trepreneurial
3000 High Expectations Way
Southfield, Michigan 48075
810-555-1122

CAREER SUMMARY

Twenty-three years of experience as an owner/executive of various types of companies including high technology, real estate/building, services, and manufacturing.

EXPERIENCE

ENTREPRENEURIAL VENTURES, INC.   **President and Founder**

Entrepreneurial Ventures *is a consulting company specializing in marketing and sales generation/growth through local, national, and international sales organizations. Client companies are start-ups through large international corporations that are in need of immediate attention and/or growth (including turnarounds). Entrepreneurial Ventures manages all phases of marketing and management of approved action plans. Entrepreneurial Ventures assists automotive, manufacturing, real estate/building, computer/software, high tech, health care, robotics, electronics, publishing, consumer products, and service companies.*

Entrepreneurial Ventures arranges Venture Capital, equity, debt, or mortgage/lease financing through Venture Strategies, Inc., an investment banking firm in Southfield, Michigan.

- Company provides Staff, Board of Directors and/or Advisory Boards with national/ international experience.

COMMUNITY OF HOMES STUDIO   **President and Founder**

Entrepreneurial Ventures financed and managed **Community of Homes Studio**, *which had the largest indoor showroom of modular homes in the U.S. (93,000 square feet), featuring ten homes, complete with landscaping and interior design, in a village-like atmosphere with pond and waterfalls. Facility also had displays, mortgage/insurance companies, employment agencies, credit counselors, builders and developers, a restaurant, and a day care center. Activities involved housing, financing, and community matters.*

- First six weeks generated 1,643 mortgage-approved buyers
- First in country to include layoff insurance for purchasers guaranteeing payment of the homeowners' day-to-day expenses; e.g., health insurance, mortgage, utilities, and day care providers
- Manufacturing capacity of sixty-two modular homes complete with site setups per week

ENVIRA CORPORATION   **President and CEO**

Research and Development Company specializing in aerospace, remote sensing, and image processing. Responsibilities included commercializing scientific projects with oil and gas companies, Department of Defense, medical institutions, and other governmental agencies. A subsidiary, a bio-tech company, was publicly traded.

- International leader in three-dimensional imaging of vision for the robotics and automotive industries.
- Leader in the monitoring of ice, icebergs, and their flows.

ZANADU INTERNATIONAL   Executive Vice-President and Co-Founder
Washington company that provided electrical and electronic components to the lighting industry. Developed strategic/business plans and managed over five hundred people in twenty-four offices throughout the United States and London, England.

- Start-up company that grew to sales of $78 million in three years.
- Sold products to over ninety foreign countries including England. 10 Downing Street was a customer.
- Rated as the fastest growing company in Washington.
- Research and development division develops products in conjunction with Motorola.

COMMUNITY CONSTRUCTION COMPANY   President and Founder
Home building company that constructed over four hundred residential homes, numerous condominiums, and several light industrial buildings in Metro Seattle. Company owned three divisions; a real estate brokerage, a mortgage company, and an equity finance company.

- Largest speculative builder in the state of Washington.
- Grew from a single real estate office to become the largest lister/seller of residential properties in the state of Washington in first three months of operation.

VILLAGE MANAGEMENT CORPORATION   President and Co-Founder
First condominium property management company in Washington. Customers included Hanson Homes, Hobbs & Cintas, Lewis & Lewis, and Allison Development. Managed maintenance, insurance, banking, repairs, construction and developer relations. Company managed over 6,000 units and expanded operations to include condominium sales.

- Expansion of the landscaping/maintenance division allowed service to thousands of apartments and commercial accounts.
- Janitorial subsidiary serviced in excess of 700,000 square feet of offices.

BENNINGTON INTERNATIONAL INC.   Vice President
Consisted of a real estate sales office primarily for used homes in Bennington - New Town, a 61,000-acre development of residential and commercial property in Lester Township, Illinois, that included an antique village (thirty-acre amusement and historical village), builders, mortgage companies, marketing and commercial/residential sales, and a community development company that developed properties in Puerto Rico and Florida.

Marketing and Sales Manager, Ohio Division. Managed three sales offices consisting of over one hundred sales and administrative personnel, New Town operations, and two other land projects in the Bloomington area. Duties included planning, land development, and maintaining municipal/homeowners association relationships.

Sales/Marketing Manager, Bennington - New Town. Responsible for all new homebuilding activities as well as commercial land sales. Duties included contracts, pricing, floor plans, home closings, builder relations, warranty, broker relations, advertising/promotion, and sales staff management.

- Largest developer of year-round single family housing in Florida.
- Developer/builder of El Conqueror Resort in Puerto Rico.
- Owner of 40,000 acres in Michigan, Florida, South Carolina, North Carolina, Georgia, and Barbados.

CHAPTER SEVEN
Using the Internet

The Internet has revolutionized the way most professionals and a lot of other people look for work, and the way companies and agencies seek employees. Failure to recognize and make use of the greatest innovation since fermented grapes may leave you out of the Web and totally unlinked.

The Internet is the fastest way to get your resume to interested parties. Aside from speed, the pros and cons of using the Internet to circulate your resume and enhance your job search are fairly balanced.

The Pros

Estimates put the number of career-related Internet sites at over 30,000; clearly online recruitment is heavily trafficked throughout the world and is a fact of life. If your resume isn't out there, you may be missing out on valuable and viable opportunities.

Contrary to popular assumption, an online resume need not differ in content from the "traditional" version. Both should contain the keywords that characterize your experience and skills; both should allow recruiters and potential employers to quickly and conveniently evaluate your suitability for their needs; and both should follow all of the other rules and common-sense guidelines that define a good resume.

The Cons

Privacy restrictions vary among sites, and your control over where your resume is posted and who can see it may be limited. The shotgun approach leaves you vulnerable to unwanted headhunters and inappropriate job leads—not to mention your current employer. In addition, any updated versions that you post may co-exist with earlier versions, creating inevitable confusion. You are advised to post your resume only on sites that guarantee tight privacy restrictions, although even these are questionable. Post updates periodically on a site that automatically deletes (or allows you to delete) previous versions, and find out if/how much they charge for updates. Remember to remove your resume from online sites when your job search is concluded.

Formatting restrictions may not allow for bold or underlined text, bullets, and other characteristics. Thus your online resume will not have the same look and feel as you might wish. Also, an online resume is not tailored toward a specific target, so you lose the ability to emphasize certain of your skills and interests over others.

Headhunters stalk the Internet, often late at night, looking for candidates with hot technical and other specialized skills. Posting your resume may get you bombarded with calls, some of which may be inappropriate or unwelcome.

The Reality

It is comforting to believe that your resume is out there making the rounds of highly motivated recruiters and interested hiring managers, but do not be lulled into a false sense of security. Online services are only additional resources, not a guaranteed pipeline to gainful employment. Continue to explore the old, traditional methods like networking, headhunters, and selected job listings.

Resources

We offer no recommendations, but some of the most popular Internet job search resources include those offered by *The Wall Street Journal* (*www.career-journal.com* and *www.careerjournaleurope.com*), and Monster.com (*www.monster.com*). You will find many resume-posting resources under such headers as *Jobs*, *Job Boards*, *Job Search*, *Resume Banks*, and various combinations of these and related words. Measure their claims with a healthy skepticism until they prove reliable.

Online Research

The Internet is as close to a perfect research tool as you are likely to find in an imperfect world. Searches that formerly took hours in libraries can be completed in minutes or seconds on the Web. If you do not have frequent occasion to use the Internet, practice by searching for different kinds of information, such as making travel plans and doing historical or geographic searches. This will help when you need to find important information.

Recognize the Internet for what it is (a great resource) and what it is not (a replacement for personal contact).

Keywords

Today's employers tend to use keywords as a preliminary step toward identifying potential candidates. This is done both on the Web and within the databases of placement agencies, recruiters, and personnel departments.

Keywords are (usually) nouns that refer to specific tools and software products like Sun and IBM; Unix and Oracle; programming languages such as C++ and SQL; certifications such as Series 7; and applications like finance, portfolio management, telecommunications, biology, transportation, and so on. You need to know the keywords specific to your job search arena in order to include the ones that belong on your resume.

There are two general techniques for including keywords: within the context of your job descriptions, and in a separate paragraph under the heading, "Keywords." If you use the separate paragraph, however, you should make it easy for the reader to find credible evidence of your keywords in the body of your resume.

E-Mail Cover Letters

The main difference between snail-mail and e-mail cover letters is brevity and format. Think of your e-mail cover letter as an abbreviation of the latter and you will be on the right track.

From the perspective of the recruiter or hiring manager who receives the letter, its purpose is to help them decide whether or not to take the time to open your resume. Most will not bother to open resumes received without a cover letter, or those accompanied by one that fails to catch their interest.

The most convenient way to write a good cover letter is to compose a boilerplate version (or multiple versions) in a word-processor. You can modify it to suit each occasion, with the advantage of a spellchecker.

The rules:

- When e-mailing your resume to a specific individual, always cover it with a letter.
- Use the subject line to briefly introduce yourself and/or refer to any previous contact (phone call, etc.).
- Elaborate with a sentence or two on the subject line message, express interest (in the recruiter or company), refer to the attached resume, and sign off with enthusiasm.
- If appropriate, briefly explain why you are writing, who referred you (or where you got the person's name and e-mail address), and one or two skills or achievements that might attract their attention.

Example #1: A Personal Promo Cover E-mail

To: Arthur C. Reese
    Southwest Tooling Research, Inc.

From: Ann Carmichael

> BOTH EMAIL ADDRESSES AND THE DATE
> ARE AUTOMATICALLY POPULATED

Dear Mr. Reese,

> STICK TO FORMAL ADDRESS, EVEN THOUGH MANY
> PEOPLE DON'T. COURTESY IS MOST OFTEN APPRECIATED.

Read with great interest recent article in Engineering Today entitled, "Southwest Tooling's Push to Maintain Engineering Excellence."

Am intrigued by your team research concept. Attached resume demonstrates my extensive, long-range commitment to tooling research and my own experience working with the team research concept.

> OK TO ABBREVIATE HERE, BUT NOT ON RESUME

Clear that you are looking for the available possible people. I feel that I can offer high degree of excellence.

Will follow up early part of next week. Hope we can arrange an interview.

Ann Carmichael

Contact Information:
100 Valley View Terrace
Santa Fe, NM 80801

home: (417) 555-4414
AnnC@overview.com

> E-MAIL COVERS ARE NOT EXPECTED TO BE AS LENGTHY AS PAPER LETTERS.
> THE IDEA HERE IS TO INCLUDE RELEVANT FACTS AND ELIMINATE THE FLUFF.

Example #2: A Cover E-mail to a Consulting Company

To: Mike Ramchip   From: Mel Marvelous
Texas Techies

Mike,

I'm a senior Web developer with Java, HTML, XML, Active X, ASP, JSP and CGI.

Have developed interactive sites for sports programs and professional team org. Resume attached.

Prefer consulting work, willing to consider full-time in Houston area.

-Mel

Contact:

100 Overland Trail   (866) 597-7777
Houston, TX 77090   Marvelocity@TTT.net

> E-MAIL TO A "HEADHUNTER" CAN BE EVEN MORE INFORMAL THAN IF ADDRESSED TO A PROSPECTIVE EMPLOYER. IN FACT, THEY TEND TO APPRECIATE THIS APPROACH.

CHAPTER EIGHT
The Art of Networking

Your resume has minimal impact on the success of your job search unless it finds its way into the right hands. Networking is one of the best ways to reach the people who can hire you, and many people consider it the most successful job search strategy available. The weight of evidence suggests that over half the people who switch jobs find their new employers through networking. All the other job search strategies (employment agencies, search firms, targeted and mass mailings, electronic networking, and opportunity advertisements) combined account for fewer positions than networking.

Guidelines

Networking is an art form rather than a science. Here are several guidelines that can help you get started in the right direction:

- Be careful not to wear out welcome mats with friends, associates, and other contacts. Schedule and pace your calls with thought and tact.
- Plan each call in detail: Write down your questions and any favors you may wish to ask. Limit these during a single call to what you would find reasonable if you were being called, and then reduce them even further.
- Be up-front about the purpose of the call. No matter how hard you attempt to mask your true intent in chitchat, they will know when you eventually get to the point, and they may resent the waste of time and deception.
- Express an interest in the person you are calling, and be sensitive to their desire to talk about things aside from the purpose of your call.
- Pay careful attention, especially if they express opinions or offer advice. You do not have to follow their advice, but avoid arguing or expressing strong disagreement with them. *You* called *them* to ask for help, and you owe them the courtesy of listening to what they say.
- If you are able to arrange even an informal interview with a decision-maker, do your homework to discover which of their needs you may be qualified to fill. Be prepared to ask intelligent and purposeful questions. Take notes, for all the obvious reasons.
- Say "thank you" at the end of the conversation—courtesy is still in style.

Definition

We define networking as:

A planned process of gathering and sharing information, ideas, and strategies through agenda-driven contacts with selected individuals in order to expand your universe of knowledge and create an awareness of your capabilities and availability.

Let's look at this definition more closely—

"... a planned process..."
Here are recognizable steps to networking that bring about the results you want. The process is "planned" in that you need to think through and design—in advance—the approaches and words you will use, and identify the people you need to contact in order to maximize your success.

"... gathering and sharing information, ideas, and strategies through agenda-driven contacts..."
Mark Twain noted that, "Reading thirty books on any one subject would cause the reader to be an expert on that subject in the eyes of most people." Networking is based upon a similar premise: Talking to a number of people who have experience and perspective in a field can dramatically increase your own knowledge. Planning up front which questions and issues to raise creates your agenda. Sharing is important—becoming a resource of information and contacts to others makes them willing to go out of their way to help you.

"... with selected individuals in order to expand your universe of knowledge..."
The people with whom you choose to network depend on the area of knowledge to which you want and need access. You may need to develop strategies for gaining entry to a particular career field or occupational specialty. If so, you would need to conduct your agenda-driven discussions with people who have an overall perspective on that field.

Example 1
A recent mechanical engineering graduate is looking for a position in computer-aided design (CAD). Her networking targets might be:

- Recent graduates who have made a transition into CAD
- Engineers who are using CAD
- Software engineers who design CAD software
- CAD instructors
- Writers, editors, and journalists in the CAD field

Example 2

An outplaced corporate manager who wants to purchase his own business feels that a franchise opportunity might be his best course of action. He should consider networking with:

- Current franchise owners—not only to determine their satisfaction with this form of business ownership, but also their satisfaction with the product or service the franchise provides
- Business brokers who buy and sell companies
- Customers, suppliers, and competitors of the particular franchise he is interested in buying
- Business and economic writers who have studied, researched, or written about franchise ownership

" . . . create an awareness of your capabilities and availability . . . "

Behaving responsibly as a person who conducts a carefully planned and agenda-driven networking program will earn you the friendship and respect of potential peers. Who better to form alliances with than people in your field of interest? Even if you accomplish no more than develop a friendly relationship with your first contacts, your time is not wasted. Often, some of the best results from networking meetings come later. The business owner you met with may pass your name on to a friend, supplier, or consultant. The more people you impress with your planned approach, the more opportunities you can expect. The universe does truly open up for those who ask—but be sure to ask politely.

Asking the Right Questions

Here's a short list of generic questions you can use to develop your own set of questions:

- What caused you to enter this field, industry, or business?
- What were your major considerations before entering this business? (for example, supply vs. demand, changing technologies, changing consumer dynamics, potential earning power, training, or upgrading of skills)
- Knowing what you know now, would you enter this field today?
- Based on what you know about me (this is where your resume comes into play), do you believe I have the necessary strengths and background to . . . ?
- Does my resume suggest enough experience to allow me to be considered seriously for this field, industry, or business?
- If so, what might I add to improve my chances for success?
- If not, what should I add or change?

- Is there anything you would recommend I do to prepare to move into this field?
- Are there any strategies I might consider to learn more about this field?
- Are there any other people you think I should contact for additional perspectives on what I'm trying to do?
- May I follow up with you at some later date to inform you of my progress?
- Is there any information about the field that I could be on the lookout for that might be helpful to you?

Avoiding the Wrong Questions

There are also pitfalls to be wary of which can destroy the most carefully laid networking plans. Avoid:

- *Criticizing a third party.* Your networking partner will consider that you may do the same to him or her.
- *Overstaying your welcome.* Stick to a time limit. "I promised to limit our meeting to thirty minutes, and I intend to keep my word." The only time it is okay to overstay your visit is when the other person suggests it.
- *Arriving too early or too late.* Always plan to arrive for the meeting with four or five minutes to spare. Earlier than that is boorish and shows bad time management; arriving late is disrespectful and inconsiderate.
- *Taking notes without asking for permission.* Always ask—most people don't mind when asked.
- *Failing to summarize the ideas, suggestions, and other names given to you.* This is the sign of a bad listener and calls into question your respect for the value of ideas given to you.
- *Asking for a job in a networking meeting.* This *faux pas* means instant loss of credibility and can be offensive to your partner. If you are offered a job (or opportunity to interview), you gain respect by politely deferring it to another time, e.g., "*I didn't come to this meeting today with the intention of asking for an interview, although I certainly appreciate your interest. I would very much like to follow up with this opportunity as soon as might be convenient for you. Thank you.*"

Be careful not to wear out welcome mats with friends, associates, and other contacts. Schedule and pace your calls with thought and tact.

Most importantly, remember to thank the other person for their time, interest, and effort.

By Letter, Phone, or E-mail?

Follow-ups can be conducted via e- or snail-mail or phone; fax and personal visits are not recommended unless specifically invited.

Unless otherwise requested or promised, phone calls may be an imposition and can lead to awkwardness if:

- The person you call does not remember you or has nothing to tell you.
- They are too busy to speak with you.
- You cannot reach them and have to leave a message.

E-mail is the recommended medium for follow-ups: Your message may be informal, arrives almost instantly, and can be answered at the other person's convenience.

In Summary

Networking takes practice. Your best bet is to begin with existing contacts who know you and may be more forgiving. However, make sure that these meetings do not turn into "old times" conversations from which you derive little value.

When you initiate a new contact, communicate your purpose clearly. Whether you were referred by a friend or associate, or found their name in a journal article or directory of some kind, identify the source of the referral, and then ask for an appointment of specified duration (no more than half an hour). Tell them enough about you to enable them to decide if they are willing to meet you. Be polite and brief.

One final suggestion that works wonders is to do your homework. Prior to scheduling your meetings, spend a few hours at the library to research at least a dozen articles of general appeal dealing with upbeat topics, solutions, and ideas that your future networking partners may find useful. These resources, which might cover technology, economics, human behavior, costs savings, customer service, and similar issues, enable you to produce timely and interesting references during your networking meetings. Imagine being able to pull out a relevant article and say, "In preparation for this meeting, I was thinking about how I might repay you for your time and generosity. By chance, I ran across this article that might possibly offer you a useful thought or idea."

Sample Letter A: Asking for Networking Meeting

JOAN A. COWEN
1234 Park Drive
Troy, Michigan 48084
(313) 689-5432

January 21, 2003

Mr. Jack Montgomery
Divisional Vice President
Armature Industries, Inc.
27777 Lapeer Road
Rochester Falls, Ml 48091

Dear Mr. Montgomery:

Loren McMasters encouraged me to contact you because of the significant involvement you have had in strategic planning. Your comprehensive ability in assembling corporate resources into a coherent plan is very important to me.

I very recently left a strategic planning position at Kalco, Inc. As you are aware, Kalco, Inc. has de-emphasized centralized strategic planning by pushing it into the line. As a result, I was given the opportunity to leave voluntarily. This led me to the conclusion that I would have more to contribute at a higher level and a significant scale with an organization that still values centralized planning.

May I reassure you that I am not asking you for an interview, nor do I expect that you even know of an appropriate opening. Rather, my interest is to gain your perspectives and ideas on those issues that may make a difference to me. Your thoughts on companies I might target would be helpful. Additionally, any contact you may have that could also offer additional perspectives would be greatly appreciated.

Enclosed is my resume by way of offering you a picture of my background. I look forward to meeting you and gaining your perspectives. Loren mentioned that you "wrote the book" on strategic planning.

Allow me to contact you in the next few days to determine when it might be convenient for us to meet.

Sincerely,

Joan A. Cowen

Sample Letter B: Requesting a Networking Meeting

Cyrus Switcher
1000 Petershaw Road
Marietta, GA 30066
404/026-1000

February 7, 2003

Ms. Charlene Cerlot
1000 Clark Street
Montreal H2 x252
Quebec, Canada

Dear Charlene,

Our mutual friend, Greg Caton, encouraged me to contact you. He felt that your thoughts on the career move you made from public accounting to general management might help me in the transition I am contemplating.

It would be helpful to me to hear what opportunities and obstacles you faced when making this transition. How you overcame the perception of "once an accountant, always an accountant" would be of particular interest.

I have known for several years that I need a broader challenge of general management in heading up a small to mid-sized company or division. Did you move into general management for this same reason?

Charlene, I am not contacting you in the expectation that you might hire me or know where a job for me currently exists. Frankly, it is your personal experience in successfully re-applying your skills in which I am particularly interested.

Allow me to call you in the next few days and see if there is a convenient time we might discuss this further. I look forward to speaking with you.

Sincerely yours,

Cyrus Switcher

CHAPTER NINE
Advice for Job Seekers

Even a perfect resume won't bring the result you're hoping for—a perfect job—if it's not used as part of a well-targeted, properly conducted job search. This chapter offers advice on several topics that every job seeker should consider before sending off a single resume.

Trends and Opportunities

Reporting on specific market trends and career opportunities is best left for Web sites and journals published on a daily, weekly, or even monthly basis. By the time a book is published, some hot areas cool and others start to simmer. No one knows for sure what the future job market holds in store, but there are ways to prepare for even this uncertainty.

Industries

Certain industries and jobs will continue to exist in some form or another; people always need food, a place to live, health care, basic services, and so on. Many, if not all banks, brokerage houses, transportation, telecommunications, and other major industries will survive the ravages of time and recession, although changes will occur to their business practices and personnel requirements.

Skills

Basic communications skills and interpersonal and management ability will not go out of style any time soon. Computer literacy is a transferable asset throughout the civilized world and elsewhere. A general knowledge of the industries in which you may be interested is easily obtainable on the Web and in libraries.

Attitude

An open mind, ability to recognize and adjust to change, and willingness to learn both new things and new ways to do old things are your best protection from prolonged unemployment or enforced retirement. Since you can't do anything about unemployment rates and the economy, don't worry about these issues and try to maintain a positive attitude. Take care of the small things, and the big picture will take care of itself.

Advice

Career consultants, employment agencies, executive recruiters, and human resources (personnel) professionals are equipped to provide up-to-date direction and advice on the latest trends and opportunities. Don't be afraid to ask.

Foreign Jobs

With a few exceptions, limit any foreign job search to places where you can speak the local language fluently. If you own a uniquely desirable and recognized talent, you may be invited by high-enough-ranking officials that you don't need a resume.

Most foreign openings available to English-only speaking people are in the sciences (research and development), technology (petroleum and communications), education (teaching), and international agencies such as the United Nations. U.S. and Canadian companies looking for people to work offshore are still U.S. and Canadian companies.

Foreign agencies and countries have diverse cultures and customs, different not only from the United States but also from one another. For this reason you should consult someone who has knowledge and experience of the place in question before preparing and sending off your resume. They may expect your CV (Curricula Vitae) in hard copy, e-mail, or handwritten; more or less detail about your job experience; and the kind of personal information that might be considered inappropriate at home. Bonne chance!

Mistakes to Avoid

Laugh if you will, but the most amazing irrelevancies and otherwise inappropriate references are known to find their way into resumes and cover letters, which then find their way into trash bins.

Rules of thumb to follow:

- *Avoid profanity and attempts at humor.* We are not entirely sure if people who write, "Yes" under Education are trying to be cute or are simply ignorant, but it happens more often than you might think.
- *Avoid personal preferences and idiosyncrasies, e.g., political affinities, preferred TV programs, favorite vacation sites, foods, etc.* Year after year, misguided folk continue to make these seemingly obvious mistakes.
- *Avoid criticisms of past employers.* What you say about others reveals far more than you think about your personality.

- *Avoid lies, gross exaggerations, inappropriate keywords, and statements that stretch credibility.* Assume that nearly everyone who reads your resume is an experienced professional capable of separating fact from fantasy. Take for granted that they will get a background check on you to verify the information in your resume.
- *Avoid abbreviations, acronyms, and at all cost, errors.* Get your resume proofed by someone reliable before you send it out.
- *Avoid the impression of arrogance, excessive humility, and other annoying traits.*
- *Avoid lengthy, wordy, difficult-to-read-and-understand tendencies and formats.* Resumes are neither experimental projects nor full-length biographies.
- *Unless you are looking for a job in the creative arts, avoid fancy, artistic, and generally unconventional fonts and paper.* The people you want to read your resume won't bother if they have to strain their eyes. Use at least 10 to 12 point type and choose between Arial, Courier, Times New Roman, or something similar.

Salary Considerations

Be aware of market conditions in general and specifically in your line of work. In a buyer's market, salaries may be lower than what you are accustomed to. If your skills are rare and in demand, you may well be positioned to ask for a premium rate.

The bottom line is to be realistic. Find out what others in your field, with comparable expertise and experience to yours, are earning, and set your sights accordingly.

Timing, demand, and location are important factors in determining salary levels. A company with dozens of inexpensive foreign workers may find your salary requirements excessive. On the other hand, if you are moving from Topeka or Bismarck to New York City or Silicon Valley, you will need to raise your expectations in accordance with a higher cost of living.

CHAPTER TEN
Cover Letters

Now that your resume has been honed into a polished gem, it's time to move on to the cover letter. This is the tool that lends your resume direction and appeal.

A cover letter is used to introduce an enclosed resume. You may be sending it to someone who has asked to see it or initiating a contact with a placement or consulting agency. You may be targeting a specific company or individual or responding to an advertisement. Whatever the purpose, the person who receives your resume expects the courtesy and direction provided by a clear and purposeful cover letter.

Objectives

A well-written cover letter meets the following objectives:

- *It offers you an opportunity to personalize and target your resume to a particular reader.* This aspect of a cover letter is one of its major strengths, since resumes are impersonal. Without a personalized cover letter, a resume may create the impression that the addressee is little more than a mass mailing.
- *It is addressed to a specific individual in the target organization, preferably someone with decision-making authority.* Most libraries have helpful resources like trade journals and directories. If you aren't sure about who's who, call the company to verify your target's name and title.
- *It allows you to direct attention to specific skills and experience.* The primary question you need to answer for a potential employer is, "What can you do for us?" Your cover letter provides the opportunity to highlight certain skills and accomplishments that may have particular meaning to your target. You can demonstrate that you have researched the company and effectively tell them, "Here I am, the candidate you've been looking for."
- *It enables you to clearly state why you are interested in the target organization.* This is the flip side of the preceding objective: the reasons you are interested in the target company. Earlier you highlighted specific skills; now you suggest where they could be put to use. Once again you reinforce the image of being knowledgeable and industry-wise.

- *It opens the door for further communication and follow-through.* The ending of your cover letter is where you can initiate the exchange of further communication, e.g., a phone call.

Writing an effective cover letter is often underestimated in the process of seeking a new job. We will contrast *how* and *how not* to do it.

Cover Letter #1a: The Wrong Way!

February 18, 2003

Ann Carmichael
100 Valley View Terrace
Santa Fe, NM 80801

(417) 555-4414
AnnC@overview.com

Arthur C. Reese
President
Southwest Tooling Research, Inc.
200 Mountain View Road
Santa Fe, NM 80801

Dear Mr. Reese, `LIFELESS OPENING`

Enclosed please find my resume. After you review it, I am sure you will find
that I'm a worthwhile and capable professional engineer who deserves further
attention. `ESSENTIALLY, SHE IS WRITING BECAUSE SHE NEEDS A NEW JOB`

My current situation no longer offers me sufficient challenges and
responsibilities. Because of this, I feel it is time to seek out another
opportunity.

If there is any interest in my capabilities, you can reach me at (417) 555-
4414. I'm positive you will find the time you spend analyzing my capabilities
well worth your time. `UNAPPEALING CLOSING`

Sincerely,

Ann Carmichael

Would you bother to read the resume attached to this cover letter if you
had a stack of resumes (in addition to other pressing documents) on your desk?
We doubt it.

This letter leaves much to be desired: it fails to include vital information,
lacks a clear purpose, and does little to entice the reader to read more.

Effective cover letters convey a sense of purpose. They project an air of
enthusiasm—regarding both the writer and the company to which (s)he is writing. They should also demonstrate the writer's understanding of the company's
goals.

Cover Letter #1b: The Right Way!

February 18, 2003

Ann Carmichael
100 Valley View Terrace   (417) 555-4414
Santa Fe, NM 80801   AnnC@overview.com

Arthur C. Reese
President
Southwest Tooling Research, Inc.
200 Mountain View Road
Santa Fe, NM 80801

Dear Mr. Reese, | SHOWS AWARENESS OF COMPANY'S ACTIVITIES AND OBJECTIVES |

I read with great interest a recent article in *Engineering Today* entitled, "Southwest Tooling's Push to Maintain Engineering Excellence." The article discussed your plans to increase your Engineering Lab Team. This emphasis on expansion appears to be a positive sign of Southwest's continuing dedication to quality service.

I am intrigued by the team research concept you have developed. The motivating force within a research team offers each member a sense of pride and accomplishment. | UPBEAT PRESENTATION |

The enclosed resume demonstrates my extensive, long-range commitment to tooling research. You will also notice my own experience working with the team research concept. It goes without saying that you are looking for the available possible people to staff your growing organization. I feel that I can offer you and Southwest Tooling substantial experience and the high degree of excellence that you need.

I look forward to meeting you to discuss your opportunities. I will call you during the early part of next week to arrange an interview and to discuss my possible involvement with Southwest Tooling. | CONFIDENT ENDING |

Sincerely,

Ann Carmichael

This version puts all four major objectives to use, stressing the writer's strengths and potential value (*tooling research and team experience*) to the company. It answers the two important questions, "Why are you sending us your resume?" and "What value can you offer us?" Then it promises to follow up with a phone call.

The overall tone is enthusiastic, informative, and confident, without being wordy or overstated.

• • • •

Not much to criticize with the following letter: Harold presents his candidacy clearly and convincingly.

Cover Letter #2: Responding to a Blind Advertisement

April 2, 2003

Harold H. Hopeful
40 Radar Street
Norfolk, VA 23510

(757) 640-4321
Hope@$$$.com

Good Day

> CLEARLY IDENTIFIES THE AD TO WHICH HE IS RESPONDING
> WITH AN AGGRESSIVE OPENING STATEMENT

The position of Chief Financial Officer, outlined in your advertisement of April 1, 2003, matches my career interests and is strongly compatible with my skills and experience.

The fact that your company is a manufacturer and distributor in both international and domestic locations is of particular interest, since these activities coincide with my recent activities.

As a Financial Officer at an international corporation, I have considerable experience in directing the full spectrum of accounting and financial management functions. Specifically, I have:

- designed and directed the installation of an international data communication network for reporting sales and marketing trends and totals;

- initiated and designed data processing systems providing significant improvement in reporting accuracy, management control, and organizational productivity during a period of rapid expansion;

- directed the cash management and treasury function (including planning and investment of $52 million), as well as all the forecasting for four divisions and fifteen markets.

> SOLID PROFESSIONAL AND ACADEMIC CREDENTIALS

Additional accomplishments are listed in the enclosed resume.

My academic qualifications include an MBA and an undergraduate degree in finance. I have been a CPA in the state of Virginia since 1992.

You can contact me during office hours at (757) 640-4321 or at Hope@$$$.com. I am looking forward to meeting you.

> UPBEAT ENDING

Sincerely yours,

Harold Hopeful

Cover Letter #3: Responding to a Blind Advertisement

September 9, 2003

Betty B. Goode
18000 Cowan Avenue
Irvine, CA 92614

(949) 660-9999
BBG@auld.com

Dear Sir/Madam,

> PROVOCATIVE OPENING STATEMENT

I am personally responsible for $56 million worth of business in five top consumer and industrial marketing accounts.

Your company is represented as one that would appreciate the special and unusual talents I offer. Do my expertise in marketing and sales, entrepreneurial spirit and professionally assertive nature appear to fit with your objectives?

> DEMONSTRATING THE ABILITY TO MARKET HERSELF

The enclosed resume itemizes my credentials as noted in my most recent performance review. My manager described me as " . . . an outstanding member of the Marketing Team who is recognized by her peers as one of the best."

Compensation is something I would prefer to discuss in confidence.

> THIS IS IN RESPONSE TO A REQUEST FOR COMPENSATION REQUIREMENTS

I am looking forward to hearing from you soon to explore any mutually beneficial opportunities.

Yours truly,

Betty Goode

> CONFIDENCE AND AN AGGRESSIVE PERSONALITY ARE STRONG SALES PREREQUISITES. YOU MIGHT AS WELL FIND OUT UP-FRONT IF THESE QUALITIES WOULD BE WELCOME.

Cover Letter #4: Responding to an Identified Advertisement

November 22, 2003

Armand G. Erwyn
(630) 910-1234
aerwyn@illini.com

2636 Forest Drive
Woodbridge, IL 60517

Human Resources Department
Fizzy Beverages
100 Skokie Boulevard
Skokie, IL 60077

Dear Sir/Madam,

I am responding to your advertisement for an Accounting Representative in the *Chicago Herald*, January 7, 2003. As the following comparison shows, my experience and background appear to match your stated requirements quite closely.

YOUR REQUIREMENTS	**MY QUALIFICATIONS**
Three to five years accounting experience.	Five years in-depth accounting experience. Achieved impressive results by reducing costs and improving inventory control. Administered five-member staff.
Strong communications skills.	Proven excellence in ongoing oral and written communications with clients and staff. Developed and presented workshops.
Knowledge of accounting systems.	Experienced day-to-day processing of complex accounting systems; generated input and analyzed output. Updated legacy system to provide greater operational flexibility.

MATCHING QUALIFICATIONS
TO REQUIREMENTS

I would appreciate the opportunity to discuss the position with you personally. To this end, I will call you next week to see when we can schedule a meeting.

Yours sincerely,

Armand Erwyn

Resume enclosed.

THIS COVER LETTER SHOWS THAT CREATIVITY AND
INTELLIGENCE CAN GO HAND-IN-HAND.

Cover Letter #5: Targeting an Executive Search Firm

October 30, 2003

Samuel S. Stats
101010 30th Street NW
Washington, DC 20007

(202) 298-8888
Sammys@bigtime.com

Ursula P. Larsson
Primebucks Recruitment, Inc.
1000 F Street NW
Washington, DC 20004

Dear Ms. Larsson,

> AN INTERESTING WAY TO GRAB
> THE READER'S ATTENTION

No doubt some of your clients are facing a problem common to many sector industries: how to stay competitive in a fluctuating market? Perhaps one of them is looking for a seasoned and broadly based executive seeking to continue a successful management career in the automotive components and manufacturing arena.

A sampling of my successful solutions include setting in motion a quality productivity program; establishing controls on raw and in-process inventories to increate cash flow; and reducing absenteeism by implementing a point system for feedback and control. I have also improved manufacturing methods to stabilize direct and indirect labor costs-to-sale ratios in the face of labor cost increases. SHOWCASING HIS EXTENSIVE EXPERIENCE

Examples:

> ACCOUNTABILITY AND MEASURABLE RESULTS

- Instituted system for in-house brazing: increased first-year profits by over $200,000 and over $400,000 over three years.
- Recommended acquisition of a company, leading to increased markets and profitability.
- Organized a tooling machine spin-off that increased parent company profits by 7%.

Further details are included in the enclosed resume. Should my background fit one of your current client assignments, I would be pleased to discuss the possibility with you.

Sincerely,

Samuel S. Stats

> AN OUT-OF-WORK EXECUTIVE LOOKING FOR A JOB.
> THIS LETTER MAKES IT EASY FOR THE RECRUITER TO MATCH
> THE APPLICANT WITH ANY APPROPRIATE OPENINGS.

Cover Letter #6: Mass Mailing

May 5, 2003

Jorge Sepulveda
23 El Segundo Terrace
San Diego, CA 12345

619/222-9999
elchefe@tamale.com

Mr. Burgess Highside
The Cardboard Box Company
23 Skidoo Place
San Diego, CA 12345

> ASIDE FROM THE PERSONALIZED ADDRESS AND GREETING, THE REST OF THE LETTER IS "BOILERPLATE"

Dear Mr. Highside,

American companies need strong manufacturing leadership that inspires their employees and delivers high quality, low cost products on time.

I have worked hard to be that kind of leader, and my customers, suppliers, colleagues, and employees would support my claim. My record over the last 12 years shows that I have built teams, raised performance, lowered costs, and delivered quality on time! More specifically:

> MEASURABLE ACCOMPLISHMENTS

- As Plant Manager of a $60-million, 400-employee high-tech stamping operation, my group was named "Plant of the Year" by *Stamping Technology Review*.

- While Manufacturing Director for solenoids and switches, I landed two of the largest customer orders in our history. Both customers placed their orders on the strength of our quality and on-time delivery record.

My Bachelor's Degree in Mechanical Engineering was earned at Ohio State University; I am currently finishing course work for the Executive Management Program at San Diego State University.

I'd like an opportunity to apply my skills in a larger organization like yours. I look forward to the possibility of discussing how I might contribute to your success. My resume is attached for your consideration.

> LOW-KEY FOLLOW-UP SUGGESTION

Sincerely,

Jorge (George) Sepulveda

> THE IDEA OF A MASS MAILING IS TO CAST YOUR LINE TO THE WINDS, DEPENDING ON WHERE YOU ARE WILLING TO WORK. BE SURE TO KEEP A RECORD OF YOUR MAILING LIST. IT IS EMBARRASSING AND UNPROFESSIONAL TO GET A CALL FROM SOMEONE YOU WROTE TO AND NOT REMEMBER WHO THEY ARE.

Cover Letter #7: Mass Mailing

August 1, 2003

Sally O'Selly
1000 East Second Street
Scottsdale, AZ 85251

480/946-6666
SOS@hotsales.com

Fight & Switch Company
2345 North Central Avenue
Phoenix, AZ 85004

Dear Sir/Madam,

> ANOTHER "BOILERPLATE," BUT WITH PIZZAZZ

The marketplace has grown more competitive than ever. New companies with new products, old companies with better products, and all with aggressive sales forces are slicing off ever smaller portions of a dwindling pie. WHO WOULD DISAGREE?

Perhaps you have experienced concern in recent months that your organization's sales force is not quite up to this level of competition. Or you may have wanted to enhance the capabilities of a pretty good group. Achieving either of these objectives requires strong and innovative sales management at the executive level. This is my reason for writing to you.

If you are concerned with sales performance, I invite you to take a close look at my enclosed resume. You may discover some qualities you might like to draw upon. Here is a brief overview of my accomplishments.

- Led my company to become the major supplier of polymer resins to nine of the top dozen users.
- Supervised the development of amorphous liquids to allow for deeper industry penetration (tripled sales in three years).
- Created a productive, harmonious sales force, decreasing sales costs while increasing sales results by nearly 45% over three years. MEASURABLE RESULTS

Please feel free to call me at the above number if you would like to arrange an interview. LOW-KEY ENDING SOFTENS THE EARLIER TONE

Yours truly,

Sally O'Selly

> FEW MARKETING OPERATIONS ARE SATISFIED WITH THEIR SALES PERFORMANCE. SALLY USES CONFIDENCE AND HIGH ENERGY TO COMPETE IN A TRADITIONALLY MALE ENVIRONMENT.

Cover Letter #8: Targeting a Consulting Company

August 18, 2003

Melvin Marvelous
100 Overland Trail
Houston, TX 77090

(866) 597-7777
Marvelocity@TTT.net

Mr. Mike Ramchip
Texas Techies, Inc.
200 Ronan Park Place
Houston, TX 77060

Dear Mr. Ramchip,

> THIS LIST OF ACRONYMS IS RIGHT ON TARGET FOR A WEB DEVELOPER

I am a senior Web developer with demonstrated skills and experience in Java, HTML, XML, Active X, ASP, JSP and CGI.

Most recently, I have developed interactive sites for the sports programs of two college and one professional team organization. My work has been called attention-getting and thorough. The enclosed resume will provide you with a detailed list of former clients and responsibilities.

My preference is for consulting work, although I would be willing to consider an appropriate full-time position in the Houston area.

> FLEXIBILITY ALWAYS HELPS

Yours,

Mel Marvelous

> INFORMALITY IS COMMON TO CONSULTANTS, ESPECIALLY WHEN ADDRESSING A CONSULTING AGENCY. MEL PROVIDES A CLEAR OVERVIEW OF HIS SKILLS AND A SMOOTH INTRODUCTION TO HIS RESUME.

CHAPTER ELEVEN
Personal Promo Letters

The personal promo letter concept is too important to leave out of a serious guide to writing resumes. Not to be confused with cover letters, which introduce and accompany resumes, the promo (also *sales* or *broadcast*) letter serves as a substitute for a resume. It is primarily used when writing to selected prospects rather than employment agencies, classified ads, and so on.

Because the emphasis of *The Resume Handbook* is on resumes, this section is intended as no more than an introductory guide to writing successful promo letters. We hope you find this brief synopsis helpful.

Purpose

The purpose of a personal promo letter is to offer a hard-hitting alternative to sending out your resume. It allows you to tailor your experience to the specifications of a position and a company. This approach can be effective when writing to a large number of corporations where you hope to attract the interest of a key decision-maker, and to explore the possibility of a current or future opening. It is not intended as a response to advertisements, especially where formal resumes have been requested.

Like resumes, promo letters are intended to obtain an interview. They are well suited to exploring corporate needs that may not yet have been defined, particularly for individuals with extensive experience and skills.

General Guidelines

Always direct your letter to a specific individual, not a nameless title. If possible, avoid Personnel and Employee Relations departments, for they are primarily oriented toward existing vacancies.

Use standard business-sized stationery, preferably personalized. Type "PRIVATE AND CONFIDENTIAL" on the front of the envelope, or a secretary may open the letter and automatically pass it along to Personnel.

Do not refer to specific past or current employers, and leave out any mention of current, past, or desired salary. Keep careful notes on all correspondence; be sure you have a quick, efficient way to locate a specific reference when someone to whom you've written calls unexpectedly.

Content

Opening Paragraph

Your opening paragraph is the attention-grabber; it has to capture the reader's curiosity and entice him or her to continue reading. Unusual, intriguing information related to your objectives is a solid bet:

- I increased the output of my department 212% while reducing billable working hours.
- I made a successful living for seven years selling African coffee in Brazil.
- As R&D Director of a major manufacturer of electronic testing instruments, I initiated the development of four highly regarded products now in production.
- How often does one have the opportunity to engage the services of an account executive who recently captured a $7.6 million contract from a giant competitor?
- My professor referred to my final MBA project in financial modeling (just completed) as "brilliant" and "innovative." He suggested that an organization of your prominence in the banking industry could certainly make use of an honors graduate like myself, following my graduation in June of this year.

Second Paragraph

This is where you tell the reader why you are writing to him/her. It identifies the specific job you're aiming for, concentrating on a specific and carefully researched objective:

- This letter is intended to explore your potential need for a bilingual petroleum engineer who is willing to relocate. If you do happen to be looking for someone with my qualifications . . .
- I am writing because I anticipated that you might have need of someone with my unusual blend of skills and experience in biomedical marketing research. Should this be the case . . .
- My purpose in contacting you directly is to inquire whether you anticipate a need for an executive recruiter with extensive contacts and experience in the academic publishing industry. If so . . .

Third Paragraph

This paragraph is intended to create interest in what you have to offer. You can state what you have accomplished in your field, or list related accomplishments that support the kind of job you're seeking. Describe outstanding achievements (from your resume) which directly support the job objective. Use short, direct sentences. Avoid boastful adjectives like "incredible" or "terrific." Cite specific figures. Don't hesitate to say:

- I accomplished / achieved / succeeded in . . .
- I have received six patents, with eleven pending, on . . .
- I saved my company $8.2 million by reducing . . .
- As Director of Marketing of a small company, I increased sales by 67% over a period of . . .
- My architectural design was selected and implemented under my direction.

Fourth Paragraph

State specific, positive facts about your education and other qualifications that can be verified. Include dates only if potentially useful to you:

- MS (with honors) in Management from the University of Michigan. I majored in Personnel Relations, and minored in Industrial Psychology.
- In 2001, I passed the 10th (final) actuarial exam for New York State.
- I authored the 120-page "Guide to XYZ Information Retrieval" (published by XYZ, Inc., 2000).

Fifth Paragraph

The final paragraph tells the addressee what action you suggest on his or her part, or what may be expected from you. Let them know when and where you can be conveniently contacted:

- It would be my pleasure to offer you additional details regarding my qualifications during an interview. You can reach me most evenings and weekends at the above number. I am looking forward to hearing from you at your earliest convenience.
- I hope to hear from you prior to June 1, at which date I am expected to make a decision as to whether I will remain . . .
- I plan to be in Chicago the week of February 2–6. In the event that you would like to arrange an interview during this period, you can reach me at my home (212/123-4567) after 6:30 most evenings throughout the month of January.

Then sign the letter.

To put these principles into practice, a self-promo example letter follows. Note that we prefer a one-page format, which is more inviting to the reader.

Personal Promo Letter: Targeting a Specific Company

October 9, 2003

Carl Corral
133 Charter Boulevard
Berkley, MI 48077

(414) 555-9876
ccorral@loa.com

Mr. Ira Azimov
Vice-President, Engineering Systems
Robotics Corporation
3333 Euclid Avenue
Cleveland, OH 44114

Dear Mr. Azimov,

> AN OPENING STATEMENT THAT DEMANDS ATTENTION. MEASURABLE ACCOMPLISHMENTS INCLUDED

In the past thirty-two months I have successfully designed, installed, and made operational a computer-controlled, visually-activated robotics system. This system has already saved my firm over $875,000, with additional savings projected to more than double that amount through 2005.

I have been following your firm's robotics efforts with great interest, especially with regard to visual scanning applications. Your pioneering innovations complement my own research and have prompted me to contact you.

> SHOWS AWARENESS OF AND INTEREST IN TARGET COMPANY

Permit me to list some personal accomplishments:

- Received the John A. Cartwright Award as 2002 Research Engineer of the Year, Michigan Chapter. > ACHIEVEMENTS THAT LEND CREDIBILITY
- Published article, "Light Shading Activators in Visual Sensing Devices," *Journal of Electrical Engineers*, December, 2000.
- Improved on-time completion of scheduled projects by 39% during my first year as Director of Research (1998), saving nearly $300,000 in early bid placements.
- Redesigned three major assembly lines, reducing downtime by 115%, reducing scrap by 55%, and improving product quality by 35%. An independent audit firm conservatively estimated bottom-line impact of these redesigns at $4.2 million.
- My MSEE was earned with honors at the University of Michigan in 1990. > SOLID ACADEMIC CREDENTIALS

It would be my pleasure to offer you additional details on how I might contribute to Robotics' future efforts in engineering and robotics research. Please feel free to call me any evening after 7 PM at home. I look forward to receiving your call.

> LOW-KEY FOLLOW-UP SUGGESTION

Sincerely,

Carl Corral

Conclusion

These principles can be applied to virtually every profession. Personal promo letters allow you to highlight elements of your background in a more personalized format and to branch off from the more traditional approaches.

Used alone or in conjunction with some of the other approaches (such as networking and the Internet), this technique can be surprisingly effective.

CHAPTER TWELVE
Following Up

The art of follow-up is overlooked by most job-searchers and can provide a winning edge when used with tact and proper timing. Follow-ups can be conducted via e- or snail-mail or phone; fax and personal visits are not recommended unless specifically invited.

There are four basic reasons for following up on an earlier contact:

1. As a simple act of courtesy to thank someone for their time, attention, and consideration, whether you are interested in pursuing matters with them or not.
2. To furnish additional information or documents promised or requested; in this case, not to follow up is an indication of unreliability or no further interest.
3. To confirm that you have forwarded certain materials, in case they got lost or misplaced.
4. To express strong interest and enthusiasm in a job, company, or service.

Convenience

- A one-page letter is the ideal follow-up to an initial e-mail contact. The receiver can open and read it at his/her leisure and may also appreciate the convenience of a clean and attractive copy of your resume. They are less likely to throw away hard copy than to delete an e-mail message, unless they really have no interest in you.
- Phone calls risk annoying busy people, especially if they have someone else on hold, and they may not remember who you are without your resume in front of them. If you leave a message on their machine or with another person, they may feel obligated to return your call even if they have nothing new to tell you.
- E-mail is appropriate for reasons 2 and 3 (above); for 1 and 4, it may be better than nothing.
- Faxes have a way of getting lost or damaged. Unless expected, don't.

Tact

If you are not expecting an acknowledgment, do not ask for one. State the reason for your follow-up and close with a polite phrase that does not attempt to obligate a response.

Good: I will be pleased to hear from you if you would like any additional information or to pursue my potential candidature for the position.

Bad: Please let me know when I should expect to hear from you.

Remember also that too much of a good thing is a bad thing; if you do not hear back from someone after an initial follow-up, wait at least two weeks before trying again. Be careful not to allow your enthusiasm to grow into an annoyance.

Each of these follow-ups is equally suited to e- and snail-mail.

Sample Follow-Up #1

April 22, 2003
RHC@rhythm.com

Robert H. Crosby
772 Memorial Drive
Cambridge, MA 02139

Mr. Tom Jones
British Sound Systems, Ltd.
4000 Hanover Street
Boston, MA 02113

Dear Tom,

> ONCE A FIRST-NAME BASIS HAS BEEN
> ESTABLISHED, THERE IS NO REASON
> NOT TO CONTINUE IT

Thank you for taking the time to meet with me yesterday.

I would like to reiterate my interest in British Sound Systems and appreciate
your willingness to forward my resume to one of the decision-makers you
mentioned.

> THIS BRIEF ACKNOWLEDGMENT SERVES TO REMIND THE
> TARGET OF HIS PROMISE TO PASS THE RESUME ALONG

Sincerely,

Bob Crosby

Sample Follow-Up #2

October 23, 2003
LyndaT@you.com

Lynda Tylor
1000 Officers Row
Vancouver, WA 98661

Ms. Agatha Kristy
Twilight Mysteries
5000 NW 334th Street
Ridgefield, WA 98660

Dear Agatha,

It was a pleasure speaking with you last week. ENTHUSIASM WITHOUT OBLIGATION

Your enthusiasm is infectious, and I hope I've done as well to represent myself as you did for Twilight Mysteries.

The writing samples you requested are attached. I look forward to the possibility of further contact. FOLLOWING UP ON A PROMISE

Yours sincerely,

Lynda

CHAPTER THIRTEEN
Other Job Search Methods

There are six other strategies that account for less than half of all job changes. These include:

1. Opportunity advertisements
2. Employment agencies
3. Search firms
4. State employment agencies
5. Targeted mailings
6. Mass mailings
7. Job fairs

A well-orchestrated search is likely to apply a combination of one or more of these strategies together with networking. In our experience, the vast majority of successful job changes we have observed, coached, or questioned used networking and other strategies in tandem. Your persistence, available time, and skill in blending them together is likely to determine how long it takes you to find a new position, as well as the quality of opportunities you uncover.

If you are employed while looking for a new job, these other strategies may be easier to place into action during nonwork hours. Their advantage is that they allow you to cover the market rather quickly and with little interpersonal contact.

However, the impersonal aspect presents a potential danger, that of relying solely on these strategies and neglecting networking altogether. We strongly caution you to avoid this lapse.

Strategy #1: Opportunity Advertisements

Today's job changers are prone to read the want ads less seriously than in the past. The prevailing view is that advertisements are a numbers game, with choice opportunity ads pulling 200 or more resume responses. So why bother? Perhaps for the following reasons:

- *Responding to an ad requires little effort.* Unless you possess unusual and obscure skills, you should be able to locate and respond to at least eight to twelve ads per week.

- *Attractive opportunity ads are more plentiful than you think.* The majority of searchers only check their local daily newspapers for opportunity ads. But trade publications, association newsletters, and national business publications are excellent resources. Most of the major metropolitan areas also have weekly newspapers and magazines that cover their local business community. A day at the local library can be an eye-opener for anyone looking for a job. This is why we urge you to read through the entire run of advertisements whenever you open the employment section. Little-known and newly relocated companies can introduce themselves to you, and interesting opportunities and potential business strategies may appear under unexpected headings.
- *Not enough experience?* Respond anyway! We encourage you to give any ad that interests you a shot. What does it cost you? Just a little paper, time, postage, and energy. If you match on even a few of the requested skills and experience requirements, your resume may snare some interest.

Blind Ads versus Open Ads

Blind ads are those in which the advertiser's name is withheld. Open ads identify the name of the company and sometimes the name of their recruiter.

Blind Ads

The most common concern in responding to a blind ad is that it may involve a company where you might be embarrassed or compromised by having your name surface as a job changer. One way to negate this potential inconvenience is to *double-envelope* your response. The inside or second envelope containing your resume will have the following message written on it.

"Please Note—if Box 123 represents the ABC Company, please destroy this envelope and contents unopened."

This suggestion is based on the assumption that blind ads draw mail first to a box at the newspaper. They, in turn, usually forward all resume responses to the unnamed company running the blind ad. It has been our experience that if you ask that your resume not be forwarded to a named company, most newspapers will honor your request.

Open Ads

Try to avoid addressing yourself to the Personnel or Human Resources department, even if this is requested. Instead, call the company named in the ad and make an effort to identify the name and title of the individual who heads the division or department where the advertised position lies.

In both cases: When responding to any ad—open or blind—do not mail a response on the first day the ad appears. Wait at least four days before you mail your response. The idea is to have your resume reach them at a time when there is less competition for their attention. Send out a second response about two weeks after the first one, adding the following note:

> "This letter and enclosed resume are my second response to your ad of (date). Please allow my double response to be an indication of my strong interest in your opportunity."

Note 1: Never send out an initial or second response to a blind ad later than thirty days after the date of the original ad. Newspapers will rarely forward boxed responses after thirty days.

Note 2: We do, however, encourage you to respond late to open ads—even three or four weeks after the ad first appeared. Many companies don't even begin interviewing and selecting candidates until several weeks after running an ad. The advice "Better late than never" certainly applies here.

Strategies #2 and #3: Employment Agencies and Search Firms

Employment agencies and *search firms* work for the folks who pay them—their corporate clients—not for you. Don't approach them under the impression that they are there to find you a job. Their mission is not to market you, but rather to locate competent individuals who match their clients' requirements. In reality, your contact with them merely adds you to the pool of people they hope to match with positions they are seeking to fill.

Which of these may be best for you, an employment agency or a search firm? The answer is based largely on where you fall in the organization chart.

Search firms tend to deal almost exclusively with mid-management through senior executive positions commanding minimum salaries of at least $75,000. If you fall into this range, consider sending your resume to several (ten or fifteen) search firms that specialize in your field.

Search firms either concentrate in your industry or field, or generalize and cover several fields and industries. They typically work on a retainer basis with a portion of their fee paid up front by the client. They may even serve as the exclusive source of candidates for a corporate client. These firms often act as consultants to the senior management of an organization. Their reputation is built on consistently providing their clients with quality candidates.

Employment agencies may also specialize or generalize. The difference is that the majority of positions handled by employment agencies are likely to pay under $75,000, covering entry-level clerical and administrative jobs up through senior technical and mid-management openings.

Like search firms, they serve their corporate clients by finding suitable candidates; finding you a job is only a byproduct. Employment agencies are paid contingent on finding a suitable candidate who gets hired. In contrast to search firms, they are less likely to be paid a retainer.

How to Use Search Firms and Employment Agencies

Timing is everything. Since most active agencies and firms only work on a few openings at a time, you need to match up your skills with their current opportunities. Your best bet is to get your resume out to a number of agencies or firms. Address it first to specialists in your field, and then to generalists.

Do your homework. Identify all of the agencies and/or search firms that cover your skills and specialty. An excellent source is *The Directory of Executive Recruiters*: www.kennedyinfo.com

This directory provides a comprehensive list of close to 2,000 search firms and employment agencies. The extensive information provided on each entry should allow you to easily identify appropriate targets for your resume. Available options include: Management Consultants, Executive Career Management, and Executive Recruiters.

Include salary information. Playing coy with firms and agencies just isn't smart. It's best to be open, honest, and realistic about yourself. Your targeted list of firms or agencies either can or cannot help you. By offering clear details about your skills, experience, and salary expectations, you make their job easier. Here are a few ways to address salary expectations in your cover letter (pick the one that most closely matches your situation).

> *"I'm very open on salary requirements at this time, as I am much more interested in challenge, opportunity, and a chance to work within the industry (or field)."*

> or

> *"I am interested in a position with a compensation package, including salary, benefits, and incentives, in the range of $75,000 to $90,000."*

> or

> *"Currently, my salary is $65,000. I am most interested in opportunities in the mid-$70s."*

> or

"Although challenge, opportunity, and the reputation of the compa-ny I join are very important, please be aware that my total compensa-tion over the last five years has placed me in the $80,000 to $90,000 range."

Identify seemingly obscure skills. Employment agencies and search firms make their reputations on finding needles in haystacks. They're in business to find people with unusual skill sets. So include in your cover letter any attribut-es, skills, and experiences that may round you off as owning a unique combina-tion of capabilities. Languages, technical and interpersonal skills, and specific project- or client-related talents and experiences can make a difference in get-ting you noticed.

Communicating with Recruiters

Don't call agencies or firms after a mailing. They can only help you if you match a job they are currently working on, and your unsolicited calls will be seen as an unnecessary irritation by the recruiter. A better bet if you haven't heard from your initial mailing is to do a second mailing three to five weeks later.

Bear in mind that search firms and employment agencies are only parts of a balanced approach. Relying on these as your sole source of opportunity is naïve, limiting, and potentially futile.

Strategies #5 and #6: Targeted and Mass Mailings

Targeted mailings are as different from *mass* mailings as laser beams from sun-light. Targeted mailings rely on concentrated and selective preparation. They emphasize *quality* over *quantity*. Mass mailings, on the other hand, operate on the principle that more is better. Like direct mail advertising, they play a num-bers game by trying to coax a response from a large-scale and relatively undis-criminating approach. Only by understanding this distinction can you hope to maximize their advantages. Let's start with targeted mailings.

Targeted Mailings

Meticulous research is required to identify people and organizations that might be interested in your unique combination of abilities. The more thorough your research, the more likely you are to identify the right target companies.

Introduce yourself to your local librarian. Be explicit about what you're try-ing to accomplish. Most well stocked libraries have a wealth of references and directories you will find helpful. Some of the better known directories include:

Dun's Million Dollar Database (Horn Library, Babson College): This and related sites of interest can be found at *http://fusion.babson.edu*. This directory lists close to 200,000 businesses in a wide range of industries such as manufacturing, communications, banking, transportation, chemicals, utilities, and retail. Within the description of each entry will be financial data, corporate addresses, and phone numbers along with a listing of the names and titles of senior executives.

Mergent Incorporated (formerly Moody's Financial Information Services): *www.fisionline.com*. Includes over 10,000 U.S. public companies and 17,000 non–U.S. public companies.

Thomas Register (Thomas Publishing Company): *www.thomasregister.com* (also see *www.thomaspublishing.com*); a comprehensive online resource for finding companies and products.

The *Federation of International Trade Associations*: *www.fita.org*

The *Union of International Associations*: *www.uia.com*

Dialog: *www.dialog.com*; online information services.

Orbit Internet: *www.orbit-internet.com*; Web hosting services

This is just the tip of the iceberg, but it will introduce you to the many excellent sources available at your local college or university library. Remember: the better your research, the better your targeted mailings. In this day and age of niche marketing, we need all the help we can get.

In summary, quality research can lead you to companies, people, and associations that are closely aligned with your skills and career goals. The extent to which you are able to pinpoint quality targets for your mailings dramatically increases your likelihood of receiving quality responses.

We've included a couple of cover letters at the end of this section to use in targeted mailings. These examples will show you how to match yourself with the target's objectives.

Mass Mailings

A well-executed job search may result in fifty to seventy-five targeted mailings; that same search could generate hundreds of mass mailings.

Mass mailings require less research, but due to the numbers involved they can result in positive dividends. Based on volume alone, mass mailings are best used by job seekers with broad skills who work in less specialized occupations.

Middle-level managers might consider doing a mass mailing, for example, to all manufacturing companies within their region or a certain distance from their home. Controllers or accounting managers could conceivably work anywhere that requires their types of skills. College seniors starting out on the job trail with an interest in sales and marketing could mass mail their resumes to the *Fortune* 1000. The objective here is to cover the market like a blanket.

To conduct a mass mailing of your resume:

Start by obtaining a mailing list. You can develop your own, which is time consuming (but less costly), or you buy one from a mailing-list company. Purchasing a mailing list can be very cost-effective in the medium and long run. A few available sources to start with are:

- Direct E-Mail List Source: *www.copywriter.com/lists*
- Polk Company: *www.polk.com*
- Other mailing and telemarketing lists: *www.marcpub.com; www.einsteinsystems.com; www.datamangroup.com*

When buying or using any existing mailing list, make sure it has been recently updated (within the past month), and that it contains the names and titles of the individuals who head up the company function appropriate to your skills and job search goal.

Address your mailings to a specific individual whose title and responsibility appear to match your search objective. For example, if you are a sales and marketing candidate, direct your letters to the Chief Sales and/or Marketing Executive; if you are an engineer, send yours to the Head of Engineering or Manufacturing. Focus on finding the best targets for your mailing. Never mass mail to the human resources or personnel area—unless you want to work in personnel or human resources.

Maintain a record of your mailing list, and keep it close at hand. Nothing is more embarrassing than getting a call from someone to whom you mailed a resume and not remembering who they are!

Write your cover letter to appeal to the largest number of employers possible. Be sure to keep track of who you send it to.

Mass Mailing Letter Example #1

May 5, 2003

George Sepulveda
23 El Segundo Terrace
San Diego, CA 12345

619/222-9999
elchefe@tamale.com

Mr. Burgess Highside
The Cardboard Box Company
23 Skidoo Place
San Diego, CA 12345

Dear Mr. Highside,

> ASIDE FROM THE PERSONALIZED ADDRESS AND GREETING, THE REST OF THE LETTER IS "BOILERPLATE"

American companies need strong manufacturing leadership that inspires their employees and delivers high quality, low-cost products on time.

I have worked hard to be that kind of leader, and my customers, suppliers, colleagues, and employees would support my claim. My record over the last 12 years shows that I have built teams, raised performance, lowered costs, and delivered quality on-time! More specifically:

> MEASURABLE ACCOMPLISHMENTS

- As Plant Manager of a $60 million, 400 employee high-tech stamping operation, my group was named "Plant of the Year" by *Stamping Technology Review*.

- While Manufacturing Director for solenoids and switches, I landed two of the largest customer orders in our history. Both customers placed their orders on the strength of our quality and on-time delivery record.

My Bachelor's Degree in Mechanical Engineering was earned at Ohio State University; I am currently finishing course work for the Executive Management Program at San Diego State University.

I'd like an opportunity to apply my skills in a larger organization like yours. I look forward to the possibility of discussing how I might contribute to your success.

> LOW-KEY FOLLOW-UP SUGGESTION

Sincerely,

Jorge Sepulveda

Resume enclosed.

Afterword

The infuriating truism that "everything is relative" can be—and often is—employed to defend some of the most eccentric and ill-conceived ideas. With regard to writing resumes, what is good and what is bad depends upon what *works*, and what does not. In the final analysis, it is the results that count.

Certainly the element of chance can help to find a great job, as is true of every aspect of our lives. But a well-organized approach can minimize the random factors and reduce the arbitrary flow of circumstances of which we may be unaware.

The guidelines and suggestions in *The Resume Handbook* are geared toward helping you increase your control over the factors governing a single aspect of your career: getting the interviews you want!

With this in mind, we've shown you the ingredients of successful resumes and included practical examples. Now you recognize the differences between:

- Relevant vs. useless or potentially damaging information
- Active vs. static
- Attractive vs. unattractive
- Attention-getting vs. dull and unappealing
- Cover letters vs. personal sales letters

You now know how to:

- Emphasize strengths and de-emphasize weaknesses
- Focus on career objectives
- Write an interview-winning resume

Perhaps some things are relative, but effective resumes are recognized throughout the business world. They are based upon the purpose and technique of carefully planned strategies. We hope that *The Resume Handbook* has helped you to develop your own strategy to get your foot in the door.

Good luck!